The NPR Curious Listener's Guide to

Celtic Music

The NPR Curious Listener's Guide to

Celtic Music

FIONA RITCHIE

Foreword by Eileen Ivers

A Grand Central Press Book
A Perigee Book

THE BERKLEY PUBLISHING GROUP
Published by the Penguin Group
Penguin Group (USA) Inc.
375 Hudson Street, New York, New York 10014, USA
Penguin Group (Canada), 10 Alcorn Avenue, Toronto, Ontario M4V 3B2, Canada
(a division of Pearson Penguin Canada Inc.)
Penguin Books Ltd., 80 Strand, London WC2R 0RL, England
Penguin Group Ireland, 25 St. Stephen's Green, Dublin 2, Ireland (a division of Penguin Books Ltd.)
Penguin Group (Australia), 250 Camberwell Road, Camberwell, Victoria 3124, Australia
(a division of Pearson Australia Group Pty. Ltd.)
Penguin Books India Pvt. Ltd., 11 Community Centre, Panchsheel Park, New Delhi—110 017, India
Penguin Group (NZ), Cnr. Airborne and Rosedale Roads, Albany, Auckland 1310, New Zealand
(a division of Pearson New Zealand Ltd.)
Penguin Books (South Africa) (Pty.) Ltd., 24 Sturdee Avenue, Rosebank, Johannesburg 2196, South Africa

Penguin Books Ltd., Registered Offices: 80 Strand, London WC2R 0RL, England

PRODUCED BY GRAND CENTRAL PRESS
Judy Pray, Executive Editor

NATIONAL PUBLIC RADIO
Barbara A. Vierow
Andy Trudeau

National Public Radio, NPR, and its logo are registered service marks of National Public Radio, Inc.

This book is an original publication of The Berkley Publishing Group.

Copyright © 2004 by Stonesong Press, LLC and National Public Radio, Inc. (NPR)
Cover design by Jill Boltin
Cover art by Dan Baxter

PRINTING HISTORY
First Perigee paperback edition: February 2005

Library of Congress Cataloging-in-Publication Data

Ritchie, Fiona.
    The NPR curious listener's guide to Celtic Music / Fiona Ritchie.—1st Perigee paperback ed.
        p. cm.
    Includes bibliographical references, discography, and indexes.
    ISBN 0-399-53071-1
    1. Celtic music—History and criticism. I. National Public Radio (U.S.) II. Title.

ML3650.R58 2005
781.62'916—dc22   2004053485

PRINTED IN THE UNITED STATES OF AMERICA

10   9   8   7   6   5   4   3   2   1

Contents

Acknowledgments

When I first traveled to the United States in 1980, I took pride in identifying myself as a Scot to anyone who asked. But if someone had probed beyond the accent for more insights on Scottish identity and how it was connected to the music I soon began to play on the radio, my answer would probably have been more than a little vague.

Growing up in Scotland in the 1960s and '70s, the matter of our ethnic identity seemed at best ill defined, and at worst still draped with the tired, old stereotypes. So back in these days, I would likely have stayed safely within practical, geographical, or even humorous explanations than to have begun dealing with the abstraction of what it felt like to be Scottish, let alone to have addressed, with any confidence, the deeper mood of identity in the nation's heart. Thankfully, a climate of change was beginning to move across the land. This atmosphere of cultural confidence was already secure in Ireland and also on the rise in Wales and Brittany. Now it's plain to see that the journey toward today's diverse, contemporary Scotland has been closely interwoven with the robust fabric of our cultural life, and especially with the growth in popularity of our evolving indigenous music and other traditional arts. Nowadays, then, if someone asked me to identify what it is to be Scottish or to be Irish, I would have plenty to say on the subject. And I would relish the opportunity to begin my answer by suggesting: First, just listen, then pick and choose from among this music to hear who we are, where we are, and what matters to us. From the recommendations listed later on in this book, I'd gladly describe who I am by offering some of the music we now call "Celtic."

Developing a concise explanation embracing all the meanings and nuances implied by the term "Celtic music" is enough to give even the most dedicated ethnomusicologist a thumping headache. With all due respect (and headache remedies) to the profession, this is not where I come from. Although I have always enjoyed reading and absorbing as much as I can about the histories and social contexts of this music, my own approach has never been wholly academic. Mostly, I take the perspective of a listener, an enthusiast, a onetime (very) amateur performer, and a radio producer and host of "Celtic" and other roots-based music programs. I am less likely to want to poke around among aspects of musical theory and technical intricacy than I am to direct my questions toward the people who make the music, to wander among the landscapes and societies that nurture it, and to wonder about its past, its future, and, most of all, its stunning emotional impact.

For more than twenty years, my weekly radio production schedule has kept me forever forward looking: planning the next show, the next interview, the next season's program themes. It goes somewhat against the grain to stop and look over my shoulder, let alone back across centuries of music making. So it's been very easy to justify not writing a book for quite a while. At last, by the endless horizons of the Lynn of Lorn, on the West Coast of Scotland, this book took shape.

A number of people have encouraged me to pause and to put together this *NPR Curious Listener's Guide*, and I'm grateful to them all. Thanks to my friends and colleagues at NPR® and throughout the public radio system for their belief in all my work, and especially their partnership in bringing well over a thousand hours of great music to listeners across the United States, and now the globe. *The Thistle & Shamrock*® has been on the air nationally for more than two decades, thanks to your willingness to provide precious air time to me and the brilliant musicians who create everything we've shared through the years. A warm thanks to all these inspirational artists, too, and to the mostly independent record labels that distribute their work: no music, no radio programs. Thank you for your creativity and incredible music making.

A million thanks to all the listeners who have journeyed with me on-air through the weeks and months and years. Your encouragement, enthusiasm, and support have everything to do with the longevity of *Thistle*, and my interest in working on this book. A special heartfelt thanks to my friend and colleague Margaret Kennedy, who has for years given so much in making the production of my program work in the special way it does, on both sides of the ocean. She was also especially encouraging and helpful during the planning and writing of this book. And to Jennifer Adams, who helps keep the operation thriving on U.S. shores, more thanks. Judy Pray served as editor for Grand Central Press, and her guidance proved invaluable to me, urging me to dig deeper.

Many years ago, Nace Toner helped plant and nourish the first seeds of what became *The Thistle & Shamrock*®. Jennifer

Roth and Doug Orr then cheerfully scattered the first seedlings across the land. Thank you, good friends all. We had no idea what we were getting into!

My parents have been silent partners in all that I've done, especially in recent radio years. Thank you to my mum, Anne, for fostering in me a love of all things Scottish, especially Robert Burns, and my dad, Robert, for giving me a good dose of self-belief and a sense of proportion! And for all the assistance you have provided in helping us raise family and radio programs, thank you both again.

And to Ian Hodgson, researcher extraordinaire, for loving support beyond measure and encouragement with great humor and insight, thank you so very much. Because all we do in preserving and extending our cultural heritage is done for those who follow, I dedicate this to our children, Eilidh and Finley, with all my love.

Fiona Ritchie

Foreword
by Eileen Ivers

"What is it about Celtic music that feels so familiar?" "I'm not even Irish, so why does this music move me?" These are fairly common questions I have heard in my travels as a professional Irish musician.

To answer these questions, you must remember that Celtic music's first home was not the world stage, but, literally, the home. It was and still is an intimate session (*seisuin*) shared around the kitchens, fireplaces, and crossroads of old Ireland, Scotland, Wales, and other Celtic regions. It was and still is the *music of the people*—the cherished gift that, in its purest form, is passed from one generation to the next. It is traditional music from these relatively small nations that has survived through the years, even when outside forces tried to stifle it. Its diaspora thrived and has influenced and merged with other forms of music through the years, thus making Celtic music ever so popular in today's continually shrinking world.

Being folk music, Celtic music touches on our shared humanity and the countless and nuanced emotions we experience every day. From the lonesome and reflective slow airs and laments, to the uplifting and joyous jigs and reels, from the cathartic, unaccompanied songs and the humorous upbeat mouth music, to the inspired and energized dance steps, Celtic music's many moods have the power to capture your ear and draw you into its heart. It is honest music, played by everyday people, and it evokes raw emotion. One can hear the history and passion of the people intertwined in these melodies.

At the heart of Celtic music is the melody—a strong, humable tune that catches your ear and won't let go. These tunes can be easily learned and passed on—in the true manner of any great aural tradition. Yet what happens within these seemingly simple melodies may be quite complex, with each player infusing the work with their own subtle yet intricate ornamentation. The result is an infinite amount of ways to play and emote a simple tune, not unlike a great jazz soloist rediscovering an old standard. However, ultimately this music is meant to be shared socially, and what fun it can be! Having a vast pool of common, traditional tunes means a Scottish fiddler from the Highlands can share a tune with a new fiddling acquaintance from the hills of North Carolina, while an Irish piper can jam with a flutist from across the world in Tokyo. The core of it all is the *seisuin* and the infectious joy on the players' faces as they share in the music and maybe even pass on a new tune to a young student of the tradition.

Underpinning these strong melodies lies the swing, the groove, that *thing* that makes you want to move. As the wonderful Duke Ellington expressed, "It don't mean a thing if it ain't got that swing." This is certainly the case in Celtic music. The subtle swells on a chosen pulse between the beats can never truly be notated, which is why listening is essential to learning Celtic music. Even the most arrhythmic listener can easily feel the overall rhythms of the tunes.

Much of Celtic music happens to be written in contemporary music's most popular time signature of 4/4. A great deal of the music also has the feel of "3," that is, 3/4, 6/8, 9/8, which is similar to our own heartbeat. Within these meters, the subtle places of rhythmic emphasis are extremely similar to those felt in African music—and by a natural progression, Caribbean music. One can even witness this marriage first-hand by visiting Montserrat, the stunning "Emerald Isle of the Caribbean," or the equally "stunning" street corners of the Bronx. In a more organic way, evidence of the universality of Celtic music abounds in Appalachian, Cajun, and Zydeco music. This effortless pairing of rich Celtic melodies and vibrant African percussion lays much of the groundwork for today's popular music.

Celtic music has never been so popular as it is today. Many musicians have discovered that incorporating complementary harmonic and rhythmic accompaniment to the raw Celtic melodies, without diluting its essence, is an exciting and accessible mix for drawing more fans to the music. Having been a part of the show *Riverdance*, I have witnessed the same exciting audience reaction to the show in nearly every corner of the world. I have been privileged to play Celtic music with old friends in the back of a pub and to new friends in the center of a symphonic stage, and the reaction is always the same. This music of the people grabs hold of the listeners and draws them in.

You might not know why you are drawn to this music. No matter what the reasons are, I am really happy that you are curious enough to have picked up this book. One thing I do know is that we could not ask for a better tour guide than

Fiona Ritchie. With her vast knowledge of all things Celtic and as the celebrated host of NPR's *The Thistle & Shamrock*® radio program for more than twenty years, she is highly respected by loyal listeners and musicians alike. But it is her enthusiastic, sensitive, smart, and fun approach in documenting all this knowledge that makes this book so enjoyable and all-encompassing. Fiona breaks it all down, from the history, to the styles and players, to the recordings we should all be listening to. Thanks, Fiona and thank you, "curious listener."

Fiddler Eileen Ivers has established herself as the preeminent exponent of the Irish fiddle in the world today. The daughter of Irish immigrants, Eileen Ivers grew up in the culturally diverse neighborhood of the Bronx, New York. Deeply rooted in Irish traditional music since the age of eight, Eileen proceeded to win nine All-Ireland fiddle championships, a tenth on tenor banjo, and more than thirty-five championship medals, making her one of the most decorated persons ever to compete in these prestigious competitions. She has played with the London Symphony Orchestra, the National Symphony at The Kennedy Center, Boston Pops, Riverdance, *The Chieftains, Hall and Oates, Paula Cole, and Patti Smith, and is a founding member of Cherish the Ladies. She's been called a "sensation" by* Billboard *magazine and "the Jimi Hendrix of the violin" by* The New York Times. *Ivers' recording credits include more than eighty contemporary and traditional albums and numerous movie scores.*

Introduction

Late in 2003, performers with the Irish theatrical extravaganza *Riverdance* packed their instruments and well-worn step dancing shoes and traveled to China. In a land where Western entertainment of any sort was, until recently, seen as subversive, this cast of musicians and dancers mounted the biggest foreign production to date in Beijing's Great Hall of the People, where Mao Zedong once presided. The show followed other recent international acts, including opera's Three Tenors and Icelandic pop singer Björk, but neither had scored a major success with the Chinese. In contrast, *Riverdance* sold more than 50,000 tickets, and two performances were added to meet the huge demand. Zhang Yu, president of China Performing Art Agents, the commercial division of China's Culture Ministry, declared the show "one of our best box office records ever."

How, then, has Celtic-rooted music from the small, wind- and sea-swept nations on the far western fringes of Europe managed to build its own global village of curious listeners? These pages offer a welcome opportunity to look at the phenomenon of today's "Celtic music," to consider its origins, to reel in the more fanciful notions surrounding things "Celtic," and to offer one candid view of a dazzling traditional and contemporary art form.

People often report that they feel transported through time when they hear the music of the Irish uilleann pipes, the small harp of Brittany, or a chorus in Scots Gaelic of women singing a Hebridean work song. In the melody of a ballad sung a capella, they hear the raw emotion of a voice speaking across the ages—universal lyrics that transcend the barrier of an ancient, unfamiliar language. Establishing this connection to something old, unique, and timeless can be a powerful experience and certainly accounts for some of the popularity of Celtic music today. Yet much of the music discussed in this book is from a recent era. Bill Whelan developed the score of *Riverdance* from a shorter work he composed in 1994, drawing influences from Spanish, jazz, and Eastern European music into the Irish mix. Its unprecedented success seems to have taken him by surprise when he remarked, "There seems to be something at its root that shows there is an acceptance of this music from many different cultures."

This music's increased visibility in the Celtic homelands may be easy to understand, as its status has risen coupled with a tide of cultural confidence and self-determination pervading all the traditional arts. For the Celtic diaspora, the music constitutes a cultural touchstone, an important means of reaffirming identity. It is also accessible to general audiences in the United States and Canada for whom its relationship to other North American acoustic forms strikes a chord. But the present, burgeoning international appeal and ever-expanding commercial viability of Celtic music far exceeds even these core audiences.

The music industry's quest for digital perfection must seem a world away to those who listen with their hearts as much as their ears and who have come to appreciate the honest emotion and passion, the unmistakable essence of community palpable in Celtic music. This is music made by people who also pick and bow for fun and friendship when they exit the stage or recording studio. For all but the best-known players, any commercial success comes only as an added bonus to a life in music. For others, it is more than enough to share and participate in a heritage about which they care deeply. A listener from any background will be quick to tune into this unmistakable sincerity and authenticity. The inventiveness, creativity, and openness that marks today's players is also attractive. Matched with breathtaking skill levels on exotic instruments, the music's power to captivate seems mostly dependent upon the performers and their recordings finding audiences-in-waiting, wherever they may be. Many people are still discovering Celtic music.

The trailblazers who have taken this music to the world are perhaps as closely identified with it, these days, as any particular national or regional variation. Young players may still be steeped in the music of their localities, but physical distance no longer restricts its reach and they are now as likely to want to emulate the sound of particular players they admire, hear on recordings, and see in concert performances. On fiddle, Ireland's Kevin Burke, Scotland's Alasdair Fraser, and Bronx native Eileen Ivers all speak in unique voices, and you can hear echoes of their personal styles in the work of emerging fiddlers, especially in the United States, where a regional flavor or influence rarely plays any role. In profiling a number of these key individuals in Chapter 5, "The

Musicians," we'll take the opportunity to delve further into their work, learning more about the wide-ranging impact of tradition bearers and innovators who have influenced the growth of the music. This may take us back in time to learn about key players and sometimes the social/historical context for the traditions we're investigating. But this is a guidebook, intended to provide an overview and pique your curiosity for further investigation. As such, you won't find here any attempt to provide a wide history of traditional or folk music, or indeed to document extensively the pre-history of the Celtic people, beyond their commonly accepted migrations and settlements. Likewise, others have chronicled the political climate of self-determination, ebbing and flowing within the Celtic nations and regions, and the folk music spawned by these movements. We'll leave further such analysis, along with explorations of the spiritual outgrowths at the fringes of this music, to spread beyond the edges of our map and within the pages of other books.

Where we will dwell, for the most part, is in the recent era of resurgence for what we have come to call "Celtic music." Dave Richardson, leader of one of the earliest bands so labeled, Boys of the Lough, recently said he credits two inventions with the worldwide upsurge in popularity of Celtic music: the home stereo and the jumbo jet. The ease of international travel, especially trans-Atlantic routes, has revolutionized the mobility of musicians in reaching unlimited new audiences. Similarly, the arrival on the market first of home stereos, then vinyl and compact discs has transformed home entertainment, as is digital recording technology and the Internet. Many of the artists highlighted in Chapter 5, "The Musicians," have opened up and expanded the musical boundaries in this era. Earlier chapters will place their work in the context of the older traditions they uphold, even as we focus upon their more recently created music.

We will also take in the music of the Irish and Scottish diaspora, primarily in North America, upon whose shores a tide of indigenous music was washed by waves of immigration in the eighteenth and nineteenth centuries. Curious listeners may need to work a little to catch the genuine voices of Scottish and Irish balladry in early country music and the rhythms of Celtic dance tunes in the old-time melodies of the Southern Mountains, on into bluegrass, rockabilly, and beyond. But there are also traditions, transplanted directly from Ireland, that thrive in the cities of the United States— on both coasts and in the Midwest—in the hands of such artists as fiddler Liz Carroll of Chicago. And in the Canadian Maritimes, fiddler Natalie MacMaster and her countrywoman Gaelic singer Mary Jane Lamond preserve and extend the indigenous music of the Scottish Highlands and Islands. No need to research the bloodlines there; the link is immediate and the spirit intact. These are living traditions developing within communities by whom ancestral culture and language is jealously guarded and sometimes, arguably, celebrated with even greater respect to origins than in their homelands.

Music from Celtic roots, played on fiddles, harps, flutes, and bagpipes and developed on keyboards, with Latin percussion, or in chamber orchestras, has never before realized the potential it does today. An unaccompanied Irish *sean nós* (old style) singer may now be seen in large venues in the United States where even the stages are bigger than the rooms in which her ballads have been shared through the centuries. Meanwhile, thousands in China can enjoy a performance of *Riverdance*, while Russians celebrate the birthday of Robert Burns to the accompaniment of Scottish fiddle and clarsach. From the pub to the performing arts center, kitchen to recording studio, this music has traveled many a mile, crossed its own seven seas, and onward it sails.

The NPR Curious Listener's Guide to

Celtic Music

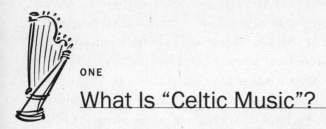

ONE

What Is "Celtic Music"?

The traditional reels, jigs, airs, and ballads mentioned in this book were lifted on the fiddles, pipes, flutes, and voices of generations of musicians before they were ever referred to as "Celtic." Fast-forward through the centuries, and suddenly we are surrounded by music identified as "Celtic," a term that conjures up a baffling miscellany of images and musical sounds. It appears in movie soundtracks such as *Last of the Mohicans* and *The Piano*, set thousands of miles from the traditional Celtic homelands. It infuses rhythmic heart and soul into the internationally successful theatrical dance shows *Riverdance* and *Lord of the Dance*. Through the music of Enya, it has inspired a luscious contemporary pop form that sells millions of albums worldwide. "Celtic" as its own category can be found in most of the major outlets for recorded music. Celtic music is in vogue. It is used to sell cars in television commercials. It has fed the fashion for another type of pseudo–New Age mysticism. Its treasures have been plundered by all manner of musicians searching for "new" music in the public domain around which to build their own arrangements (sometimes without acknowledgment to the source!). It is, we could easily claim, a cynical marketing strategy employed by some corners of the recording industry, who find that sales increase when "Celtic" appears on the label, though the music may lack the merest shred of authenticity. In fact, retailers in all sectors are lining their pockets on the back of the "Celtic" label. Ethereal and romanticized "Celtic" images and sounds are regularly packaged around highly marketable commodities. The frenzied feeding of the Celtic brand shows little sign of abaiting.

But surely Celtic music is much more than any of this. Can we cut through the hype of conflicting messages to reach the pure essence of the music? How do we capture its true spirit? What about its authentic roots, the genuine and unique continuity of traditions from which it grew, and its amazing longevity? Where does all this merge with the contemporary cross-cultural environment that sustains it today and the ascent of the term "Celtic music" over the past three decades or so?

In this book, we will try to answer some of these questions by rambling across well-trodden terrain. For our purposes, we place "Celtic music" among the traditional and evolving indigenous musical cultures of the so-called Celtic countries and regions: Ireland, Scotland, the Isle of Man, Wales, Cornwall, Brittany, and Galicia and Asturias on the Spanish coast. The main instruments, styles, and forms of the music will all be explored. Songs and singing in Celtic languages, especially Irish, Scots Gaelic, Welsh, and Breton will be considered, too, along with the rich heritage of songs—old and new—in the hybrid language of Scots. And we'll follow the music from the old world to the new.

In attempting to define Celtic music, it's important not to

get too bogged down by the definitions. Pieces of music don't come with zip codes, and sometimes locating music as "Celtic" has as much to do with its feel as with its specific origins, which might be quite varied. For example, traditional music in Scotland has its roots in Celtic, Anglo-Saxon, and Norse cultures, determined by whether the music originates in the west, south, or north of the country. Irish music may be traced to a bardic heritage, first nurtured by the Normans who invaded and settled in the twelfth century. The Welsh attribute their music to the ancient Britons, Celts who retreated westward, as do the Cornish. The music of Brittany, closely and consciously linked to Wales, Ireland, and Scotland, has also evolved within a French setting and provides a Celtic/continental link. In the Spanish regions of Galicia and Asturias, this bridge has an even wider span into European musical influences. So it makes sense that Pan-Celtic musical festivals from Europe to North America highlight as many musical differences as they do similarities between the different so-called Celtic traditions. What is often being celebrated at these gatherings is a feeling of connection, a veneration of tradition, a love of community, and an investment in a shared ancient history. It is a belief, if you will, in the bond of "Celtic" identity as it is expressed through music.

Another issue to be settled concerns the definition of traditional music. Where does it begin and end? In the mid-seventeenth century, the fiddle replaced the viol (an early type of violin) in the Scottish court, and by the eighteenth century, aspiring players in all levels of society were buying fiddles. Dissenters could have stood up and yelled, "Wait a minute, we can't have this fiddle rubbish polluting our music. It's not traditional!" Had they succeeded in their plea, Scotland would have lost one of her three national traditional instruments before it even got going. And what could have more hold on our view of Scottish traditional arts than the repertoire of the bagpipes? Yet there was a time when 2/4 marches were considered "untraditional" in piping circles. Now they are at the core of every piper's tune set. Through Irish music, the African American banjo and, more recently, the Greek bouzouki have been added to the accumulation of instruments we now expect to see in a contemporary Celtic music band playing "traditional music." Speaking of which, these multi-instrumental lineups, often with featured singers, are also a relatively recent invention. We could easily cite many more similar examples from across the ages.

If it is to survive and thrive, traditional music cannot be allowed to ossify. Thankfully, within the realms of Celtic music, it never has. We must nonetheless find some way to separate music that is genuinely traditional from innovations that depart from the root and branch out anew. It is easy to identify as "traditional" any pure musical performance that strives to be true to an inherited style: an unaccompanied Scots Gaelic song from singer Christine Primrose or a set of jigs played by master Irish fiddler Tommy Peoples. These are distinguished traditional performers by any measure and have motivated others who are inspired by their great gifts. So for any music to qualify as traditional, it must surely have an unbroken linkage with the past. Although creative innovation and expanding repertoires are very much welcomed, it's not always about progress for its own sake.

Usually traditional music will have evolved through the process of oral transmission, having been absorbed, sometimes unwritten, into the community as a living popular culture. Essential for a living tradition, it might vary or change dramatically, through the novel approach of the individual performers. And it must, in turn, be absorbent enough, over time, to soak up new tunes and songs created along traditional lines. Prolific composers of today, such as Highland piper Gordon Duncan and fiddler Liz Carroll, will already see their tunes listed alongside the anonymous "trad.arr" credit in many recordings of traditional music. But let's agree that there must be something about a more experimental arrangement of traditional or recently written material that remains essentially true to its musical roots for it to be fairly considered "traditional" in style. And it needn't necessarily be classified this way. Sometimes it's best to call music simply "new," even if it still wants to be known as "Celtic." Much of the music presently gathering under the Celtic umbrella has an evolving momentum supplementing its more traditional inspiration. Celtic music is clearly not synonymous with traditional music.

Where does all this leave rootsy rock outfits like Ireland's Hothouse Flowers or Sinéad O'Connor, who presented her first recording of traditional standards, *Sean Nós Nua*, in 2002? What about Big Country and The Proclaimers from Scotland, rock/pop bands popular in the 1980s and '90s to which music reviewers often attributed a latent "Celtic" or "folk" influence? Any well-tuned ear can pick out the vocal nuances from traditional singing styles in some contemporary Irish bands and artists, and there's an echo of the drive and passion from piping or folk song detectable in Scottish ones. None of these artists would accept the label "traditional," but is their music "Celtic"? What about groups like The Corrs, weaving Irish jigs and reels and traditional melodies into their brand of pop, or Scots singer songwriter Eddi Reader, who has recently applied her unique voice and imaginative arranging skills to the songs of Robert Burns? Perhaps this is something you might want to decide for yourself, as you listen to the hybrid miscellany of new sounds and textures.

Here are a few suggested distinctions that might help you: For *traditional* musicians, connecting with the origins of their music is the priority; for artists identifying themselves loosely as *Celtic,* it's perhaps only a matter of interest while they explore other avenues for their music. While traditional or Celtic influences sometimes percolate the music of bands like Hothouse Flowers, they seem to do so more as a by-product of the commercial writing process. The "Celticness" is suggested more by the artists' own ethnicity and interests, rather than being a primary inspiration for their music. Don't strive too hard to be overly inclusive with what is already an imprecise labeling art. And remember, too, that placing music in pigeonholes has always been of much more the domain of record labels, retailers, reviewers, and radio programmers than it has ever been to musicians. An artist may have no interest in thinking herself "Celtic," let alone "traditional," and then create one album that sits comfortably aside others we would identify as core Celtic recordings.

Regarding "traditional Celtic music," we could query whether such a broad banner is ever appropriate. Although we might point out that fiddles or small harps are commonly played wherever we find this music, each of the Celtic nations and regions has its own set of musical traditions, customs, forms, styles, and even unique instruments. Some artists have followed the path forged by Breton harper and world music pioneer Alan Stivell and taken a Pan-Celtic approach to their music, combining melodies from across the "Celtic lands" within their arrangements. But most do seem to stay largely within their own traditions, even as they experiment with contemporary stylings and borrow from the world's library of music. For those reasons, you will notice that something is likely to be identified in this book as "Irish," "Scottish," "Welsh," or "Breton" rather than falling back on the catchall

"Celtic." Perhaps the "Celtic music" label is at its most useful as we categorize hybrid forms, and contemporary music that draws upon indistinct Celtic traditions or uses them as a starting point before consciously blending them with other influences. Or when we simply want to talk about lots of music, from across Celtic traditions old and new, on compilation albums, on radio programs, and in books like this one.

Despite the blurry and limited usefulness of the "Celtic music" label, we can and must distill the essence of musical identity in the different landscapes and languages through which all these great songs and tunes evolve. Ultimately, labels and categories should be surplus to requirement—it is the heart and soul of the genre that this companion seeks to embody. Then hopefully, without really noticing, you can emerge from the other side of this book having left the categories within the cover. May you come to a persuasion that what this music does share, across accepted Celtic traditions, contemporary innovations, New World variations, and cross-cultural collaborations, are qualities that speak directly to our shared humanity. May you then touch its essential spirit, washing over you on an emotional level, effortlessly provoking feelings of joy and hope, sadness and reflection in the trill of a flute, the rasp of a fiddle, the lilt of a pure singing voice. If you can close this cover again, lay aside its histories and luminaries, and meet the music on an intimate, personal level, then you'll have grasped its timeless essence, universal appeal, and beauty.

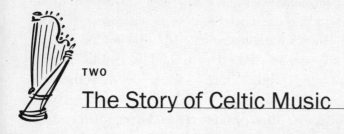

TWO

The Story of Celtic Music

Ancient civilizations surface in antiquity, rather than arriving at a particular place and time. So the people the Greeks called "The Keltoi" emerged from prehistoric homelands somewhere in Central Asia around 1000 B.C.E. A French definition states that prehistory stops with the first written document. Because they left no written accounts of themselves, the Celts certainly qualify as a prehistoric people; however, they were technologically skilled and gathered in sophisticated societies. In time, the spread of the Roman Empire would help to blur the distinctive identities of these groups, but they were actually a miscellaneous collection of tribes with some common attributes in their languages, the art they created, and the customs they observed. They were nomadic, eventually creating communities all across the European continent. By the fifth century B.C.E., they had spread through Bohemia and Austria and into Germany, France, and Italy. Around 390 B.C.E., Celtic Gauls even sacked Rome, but they were not alone in their conquering, migrating ways. The powerfully expansive Roman Empire eventually suffocated the entire continental Celtic world, except for areas north of the Rhine and Danube. These lands were soon overrun, however, in the first few centuries C.E., by other ethnic groups: successive invasions of Goths, Huns, Vandals, Franks, Angles, Saxons, and others who obliterated what may have survived of the original Celtic societies there.

Meanwhile, well off the beaten track, the so-called barbarian tribes of Caledonia (northern Scotland) remained fiercely independent of all these forces, while Ireland was never invaded by the Romans. As the Roman Empire fell into decline in the third and fourth centuries, the remnants of free Celtic tribes reasserted themselves. The Picts emerged as dominant in Scotland, and sea traders from Ireland known as Scotti began to control western coasts. Anglo-Saxon invaders flushed native British tribes into what we now call Wales and Cornwall. About 1,500 years ago, British Celts voyaged southward across the sea and invaded Armorica, now Brittany in Western France. During a similar era, Celtic peoples also arrived from the area of the Rhine and upper Danube valleys and mingled with the existing population of the Spanish Iberian peninsula. In time, Ireland, Scotland, Wales, the Isle of Man, Cornwall, and eventually Brittany in France and Galicia and Asturias on the Spanish coast were held to have endured as Europe's "Celtic Fringe." These ancient Eurasian migrations are why the Celts' archaeological pathway stretches from the Balkans to Ireland.

Here, then, is a very rough sketch of several centuries of highly complicated social history, migration, and warfare. This potted history offers one simple overview, or perhaps one set of beliefs, about the origins of present-day Atlantic Island and Continental Celts. Does that mean we can stretch those assumptions toward an assertion that the people who today call themselves ethnic "Celts" have maintained their identities and cultures unchanged for more than 3,000 years? And is what we call "Celtic music" a preserved collection of melodies and styles passed down across the millennia from the forefathers of European civilization? Well, not really.

Some music forms can certainly be traced back to ancient times, especially among the Irish and Scots Gaelic song traditions, where ballads recall the exploits of seafaring heroes of the third and fourth centuries. The small harp has been made and played in Scotland since at least the eighth century, when its image was hewn onto Pictish stones dating from that era, and a ninth-century woodcarving in Ireland depicts a piper. *Piobaireachd,* or *ceol mor* (big music), the so-called "classical music" of the Highland bagpipes, dates back to the 1500s, when it was invented by the MacCrimmon family, hereditary pipers to the Clan MacLeod on the Isle of Skye (see Chapter 3, "Varieties of Celtic Music"). However, most of the instrumental music we today call "Celtic"—the reels, jigs, hornpipes, and strathspeys— is dance music dating back little more than three centuries.

William Jackson, Scottish composer, harper, and multi-instrumentalist, proposes that if you really want to sample true "Celtic" music, the proper course of action would be to investigate the sound of the carnyx: the tall, periscopelike war trumpet of the old-world Celtic tribes. This authentic ancient, hair-raising instrument even made the Romans nervous. It has been rebuilt in recent years, complete with the boar's head through which the eerie notes bellow. Trombone player John Kenny plays one, and its haunting cry is paraded in some of William Jackson's music, including his epic suite *Duan Albanach.*

To heap on more controversy, there are even archaeologists

who challenge the orthodox identity of Celts in Britain and Ireland in light of new research on Atlantic Iron Age peoples. It is accepted that Britain had been receiving Celtic peoples in small tribal bands for centuries. Julius Caesar certainly wrote of the "Belgic immigrants who come to plunder and make war" at the time of his first attempted landings in Britain in 55 B.C.E. However, some scholars question the long-held belief that European Celts eventually launched major overwhelming migrations to Britain and Ireland and suggest that more ancient indigenous Stone Age peoples, no doubt in contact and exchange with Continental Celts, are the true ancestors of today's "Celts" of Britain and Ireland.[1] Indeed, there is no evidence that anyone in these lands ever referred to themselves as "Celtic" until after 1700. This is clearly fodder for a fiery debate by itself, with untold implications for our assumptions about "Celtic music."

As civilizations emerge from their distant past, rather than arriving at a discrete place and time, so, too, does their music unfold across the ages and down the generations. It does so via the only available technology: oral transmission. Unlike an art form such as opera, which was conceived at a particular point in history, the music we now call "Celtic" has evolved across cultures, through countless generations, social conditions, and political forces.

And onward it flows, from many tributaries, in a wide, meandering current. So there really is no one story of Celtic music. Rather, the music has been hewn by comparable forces that have acted since the dawn of time on the related cultures now identified as Celtic. It would be speculative at best to attempt to unravel the countless threads of musical history

---

[1] Simon James. *The Atlantic Celts: Ancient People or Modern Invention?* Madison: University of Wisconsin Press, 1999.

from ancient times through the dark ages. A more instructive approach would be to consider some broad trends from more recent times that have given birth to what appears to be a coherent set of related musical traditions recognized throughout the world as "Celtic."

Ireland and Scotland: Winds of Change

It would be unwieldy to generalize across all the cultures on our map, so we will narrow our focus here to say that parts of Ireland and Scotland in particular were buffeted by similar cruel winds of change. This has had a bearing on the history of all the music. Both countries supported a system, over a period of centuries, where the clan chiefs and other gentry patronized hereditary resident pipers and itinerant musicians, mostly harpers, who would visit their homes in an extended grand tour. These societies were destroyed in times of great strife and suffering. In Ireland, English colonization began under Henry VIII in the sixteenth century, and by 1640, Cromwell's soldiers were routing out harpers, pipers, and other wandering musicians. Support for their lifestyle dwindled with the disappearance of their patrons, so that Turlough O'Carolan (1670–1738) became known as the last of the Irish Bards. In Scotland, much the same happened in the aftermath of Bonnie Prince Charlie's failed 1745 Jacobite Rising against the Hanovarian crown. The system of patronage, under which much traditional Highland music was written by such historical figures as harper Rory Dall Morison (1656–1713) was destroyed. The wearing of tartan was even banned by the British government. Bagpipes were first banned, then appropriated as a rallying instrument to bolster the ranks of the British military, and were to become associated for decades with military bands and Highland regiments.

Last of the Irish Bards

After years of war for control of Ireland, a delicate peace was holding when Turlough O'Carolan (1670–1738) was born into the peasant class in Roscommon, a county in the Province of Connaught in the West of Ireland. The struggle against colonization had raged since Henry VIII began the plantation system in the sixteenth century. By 1670, the ancient harp, once played throughout the land in the courts of chieftains and kings, was making a quiet comeback in the homes of the landed gentry. For such a gentle instrument, it had only recently still been held as a subversive symbol of the Irish national spirit. The 1640s had seen Oliver Cromwell's troops ruthlessly track and kill harpers and destroy their instruments, just as the army of Elizabeth I had done sixty years earlier.

Although no longer outlawed, the status of harpers was very much diminished when Carolan began his musical career in 1691. Smallpox had robbed him of his sight at age eighteen. This was the fate of one third of those who survived the disease, and it proved to be the turning point in Carolan's life. The MacDermott Roe family, on whose estate he worked, supported Carolan in studying harp so he could make his living playing in the big houses of the few remaining wealthy landowners.

When he took to the road at age twenty-one, a novice at his new trade, Carolan would have been expected to recite, sing, and compose for his patrons, the remnants of a ruling class for whom the harp was such a beloved bond to a more glorious past. On his first outing, his patron wasn't too impressed by the young Carolan's playing and suggested he might do better to compose. Although he couldn't read or write music and had no formal training in composition, Carolan composed more than two hundred melodies in his lifetime, some of which he named *planxtys,* or tributes to his many patrons. His work stands today as a bridge to the past, a unique link between the baroque-style European art music of his day and the ancient bardic traditions of Irish harp music.

Traveling, playing, and composing for his patrons for almost fifty years, Carolan is remembered as the Last of the Irish Bards.

The first recording of Carolan's music wasn't made until well over two centuries after his death. In the early 1960s, Seán Ó Riada formed the first Irish traditional instrumental ensemble, Ceoltóirí Chualann, from which The Chieftains sprang. In 1967, Ó Riada and Ceoltóirí Chualann recorded three Carolan compositions on their album *Ceol na nUasal*. The Chieftains' second album, *Chieftains 2*, also featured a Carolan melody in the same year. It was the snowflake that triggered the avalanche. As a direct result of the vision of Ó Riada, and the international popularity of The Chieftains, Carolan's music has been presented to an international audience. His debut composition, "Si Bheag Si Mhor," has now been featured on well over one hundred individual recordings from Ireland, the United Kingdom, the United States, and beyond. In the twenty-first century, Carolan's reputation only continues to grow.

In the eighteenth century, the fiddle surfaced as the social instrument of choice in Scotland and Ireland, along with cello and flute. Legendary players and composers such as Niel Gow became prominent during this era, and their legacies still influence musicians. The fiddle was ideally suited for dance music at community gatherings, marking weddings, wakes, local festivals, and filling the ballrooms of the landed gentry, some of whom assumed the old role of musical patrons to the best fiddlers. But before the early part of the last century, the idea that traditional music would some day be performed on a stage before an audience could not have been further from the minds of those eighteenth-century fiddlers and dancers alike. What had to occur to where this music was embraced as both community activity and performance art?

Perthshire's Pride

Niel Gow (1727–1807) was born at Strathbraan in Perthshire, Scotland, in the heart of a region celebrated for its many outstanding fiddlers and composers. His father was a weaver and moved his family to a cottage in the village of Inver, near Dunkeld, when Gow was a youngster. Gow started playing fiddle early, won his first competition at age eighteen, and was soon to be hailed as the finest fiddler of the day. With his brother Donald often accompanying on cello and a string band of other well-known fiddlers and cellists, he became a favorite at dances throughout the countryside and especially at balls held by the aristocracy. The Duke of Atholl was Gow's chief patron. He developed a long-standing friendship with the fiddler, whose sharp wit and good nature were legendary.

Gow was visited by many historical figures of his time, including Prince Charles Edward Stuart (Bonnie Prince Charlie), writer James Hogg, and, most famously, Robert Burns. Burns traveled to Perthshire to meet with the fiddler and hear some of his tunes, writing verses to commemorate their encounter:

> Wha doesna joy to hear the ring
> O' ilka bonny lilt and spring
> That ye frae recollection bring
> And wheedle through your fiddle?

Niel and his five sons were involved in collecting a great amount of Scots fiddle music, publishing ten volumes in addition to their own compositions. Nathaniel Gow was the best known of Gow's sons. Like his father, he was patronized by the nobility for whom he often played, reputedly eventually receiving a pension from George IV.

Of all the tunes Niel Gow composed, perhaps the most well loved is the tune he wrote in honor of Margaret Urquhart, whom he married in Perth in 1768. Niel Gow's Lamentation for the Death of His Second Wife, often cited as the most beautiful fiddle tune ever written, can be found today on recordings from Scotland to North America, along with many more Gow compositions (see Chapter 6: "The Music").

Bound for America

In nineteenth- and even twentieth-century Ireland, the pipes or fiddle would always be brought out to toast the departing emigrant at his or her American wake, a send-off ceilidh for a loved one who might never again step on Irish soil. Although blending fun and sadness, an American wake symbolized the death of the person traveling, and gatherings such as these represented a trend that almost sounded the death knell for Irish music itself. Ever since the Elizabethan conquest of Ireland, the country's chief export had been people. With the Great Famine of 1845–47, the floodgates opened and two million left in the ensuing decade. At least a million had already departed even before the onset of the Famine, and one and a half million died at home in this "Great Hunger." Many tens of thousands were also transported to Australia in the early decades of the nineteenth century, sentenced for "crimes against the crown," which might range from petty theft to political dissension. By the early twentieth century, a further four million chose to sail away, mostly for North America. The effect on Irish cultural life from this loss of Irish men, women, and children was incalculable.

Scotland, too, saw a waning of interest in the music as the notorious Highland Clearances took their toll in the nineteenth century. Landlords, many of whom were clan chiefs to whom their tenants had demonstrated remarkable loyalty for generations, depopulated their lands to make way for something more profitable: sheep. These mass enforced emigrations took huge numbers of Gaels to the Carolinas, Nova Scotia, and beyond. And vast numbers of Lowland Scots have been economic migrants from the seventeenth century to the present day. Scots had always made a disproportionate contribution to the exodus from the British Isles, but in the nineteenth century alone, at least two million Scots emigrated. Nevertheless, the core of the music and its regional flavors managed to remain intact, from the Norse influenced fiddling of Orkney and Shetland, to the agricultural ballads of Aberdeenshire, the gritty urban street songs of Glasgow and Dundee, and the epic Border Ballads. The songs of Robert Burns, collected and written in the Scots tongue, have been a passion for Scots since they were first published in the eighteenth century.

However they, and the fiddle music, had to survive another eroding force: the Victorian gentrification of the instrumental and song traditions lasting well into the twentieth century.

Burns Night Celebrations

Each January 25, people congregate in town halls, hotel function rooms, and pubs throughout the world, united by a celebration that transcends their political, religious, and social differences. Their evenings culminate in an anthem of friendship, penned in words many will only partly understand. It is the same chorus sung universally to herald the beginning of each New Year. And it all serves as proof that no one has spread Scottish music around the world as successfully as Robert Burns (1750–1796).

January's Burns Night celebrations mark the birthday of Scotland's National Bard. They follow a set program of music, dining, toasts, poetry recitation, and often laddish innuendo about Burns's love of life and of women. But rarely do they recognize the man's major contribution. Poems and original songs apart, Robert Burns was the foremost collector and arranger of traditional Scottish songs. The product of this labor of love was *The Scots Musical Museum, 1787–1803,* by Robert Burns and his co-editor James Johnson (later George Thomson). In collecting and extending fragments of traditional verse for these five volumes, and in preserving old melodies by using them for his songs, this obsession in life and bequest has had immeasurable impact on Scottish musical heritage and culture. As singer Jean Redpath says, "He was a walking encyclopaedia of Scottish music. If you're looking for a ballad, a drawing room song, or a dance tune with four sets of lyrics, you'll find it in Robert Burns. If you're looking for comedy, tragedy, political satire, or social commentary, you'll find it in Robert Burns. No matter what it is you want to express, no matter how you want to express it, you don't have to look any further than Robert Burns."

The last century saw several attempts to collect and arrange the songs of Robert Burns, including the work of the late Serge Hovey, an American who devoted years to researching and setting the 323 known Burns songs to their original melodies. His collaboration with Jean Redpath resulted in six volumes of his arrangements being recorded by the Scots singer. These were released on the Philo/Rounder label.

In 2002, Dr. Fred Freeman completed his project of recording all the songs for the thirteenth-volume *Songs of Robert Burns,* released by the Scottish label Linn Records. The collection, begun in 1995, was intent upon offering the songs in their most natural musical settings, with the clarity and simplicity so highly valued by Burns. These volumes are a remarkable recorded document of one of the world's great musical collections. In striving to do justice to the spirit of the songs, they have also succeeded in bringing together a generation of some of Scotland's finest singers. These include Rod Paterson, James Malcolm, Christine

Kydd, Gordeanna McCulloch, Jamie McMenemy, Corrina Hewat, John Morran, Elspeth Cowie, Karine Polwart, and the sorely missed voices of both Davy Steele and Tony Cuffe.

Burns had a profound sympathy for both human and animal kind, was much loved, and transcended the harshness of life on the land to become an international poet of the people. His original songs and settings of traditional verses have never been more popular than they are today. From traditional singer Sheena Wellington, to contemporary singer songwriter Dougie MacLean, there are few Scottish artists who do not include his works on at least some of their recordings. In his life's work, he changed the course of folk song in the British Isles and beyond, leading individuals from well outside the Scots song tradition such as Ralph Vaughan Williams to declare, "There can be no more original genius than Burns."

Hands Across the Water

While emigration depleted musical communities in Ireland, these grew and thrived in the cities of the midwest and eastern United States. In the late nineteenth century, the Chicago chief of police, a native of County Cork, founded a society of Irish instrumentalists and set about collecting tunes from emigrants to his home city of Chicago. Francis O'Neill's collections eventually contained nearly two thousand traditional tunes and became the main source of Irish music in the United States and, importantly, back home in Ireland, where they found their way into many homes. After decades of ebbing away, the music was at last flowing back to the source.

In more recent times, a similar return of long lost riches has infused Scottish music with new energy. As part of the widespread and detested Highland Clearances, landlords in the Scottish Highlands oversaw the eviction of thirty thousand men, women, and children, transporting them to Cape Breton Island, Nova Scotia, in the first half of the nineteenth century. They were following in the stead of some twenty thousand who had made that same crossing in the 1760s and '70s, escaping crippling poverty and rising rents. They brought with them their Gaelic language and songs, their dances, and their distinctive style of fiddling. These elements of Gaelic culture were preserved by intervening generations on Cape Breton, even as they may have changed and drifted in Scotland. Since the 1980s, cultural custodians such as Cape Breton fiddlers Buddy MacMaster, his niece Natalie MacMaster, and her cousin Ashley MacIsaac have visited Scotland, the birthplace of so many of their tunes, and reminded players there of a more raw, dance-driven fiddle style than now predominates in Scotland. The stream of musicians flows freely in both directions between the two lands today.

Cape Breton's very isolation allowed the islanders to maintain, over the past two centuries, a continuous tradition and fluency in Highland fiddling from a golden age of Scottish music.

The Captain from Chicago and The Book

Daniel Francis O'Neill (1848–1936) of County Cork left his home near Bantry Bay at the age of sixteen. As the story goes, he was carrying a letter of introduction to the Bishop of Cork City, but instead secured a position as cabin boy, sailing to England and onward to Russia, Egypt, the West Indies, South America, Hawaii (where he survived a shipwreck), and Japan. When he arrived in the United States, he herded sheep in the Sierra Nevadas and taught school in Missouri. Eventually he settled in

Chicago, working as a railroad clerk and a lumberyard supervisor, before joining the Chicago Police Department at the age of twenty-two. O'Neill rose steadily in the ranks until 1901, when everyone came to know him as Chief O'Neill, General Superintendent of the Chicago Police Department. Wherever he traveled, O'Neill had always carried his passion for traditional music along with him, memorizing hundreds of melodies. He was a fine flute player, who could also lift a tune on fiddle and on Highland and Lowland pipes. Although he settled many miles from Ireland, O'Neill could hardly have been in a better place than nineteenth-century Chicago to expand his musical interests. By the time he arrived there in 1873, forty thousand Irish immigrants from all thirty-two Irish counties were living in the neighborhoods of Greater Chicago. By the turn of the century, the figure had soared to almost one quarter of a million.

Chief O'Neill began to seek out musicians from the Irish strongholds, collecting and transcribing tunes he may never have heard had he remained at home, making sure he extended his efforts to the constant stream of visiting musicians who passed through the city. "Nobody, unless one has seen and also felt it, can conceive the inexplicable exhilaration of the heart which a dance communicates to the peasantry of Ireland," he enthused. By the early 1920s, his tune collecting had yielded nine volumes, five of which he published with his own money. Collectively, they became known as *The Book,* the largest collection of traditional Irish dance music ever published.

Francis O'Neill spent more than three decades dedicated to his cause, even leaving the police force in 1905 to apply himself full-time to his labor of love. When his books found their way back to Ireland, they served as an inspiration to a musical community struggling to survive the aftermath of mass migration and social scorn. O'Neill's collection represented the twentieth century's most important individual effort to preserve Irish music. *The Book* is rightly credited as having made a vital contribution to Irish culture throughout the world.

The Recording Era

By the turn of the twentieth century, an invention was being refined that has more to do with the widespread popularity of Celtic music than any one instrument: Thomas Edison's recording machine. The recording companies Columbia and Victor were making Edison wax cylinders and Berliner flat discs commercially available for the first time. Piper Billy Hannafin was one of the first Irish musicians to be recorded on wax cylinder in 1898, and vaudevillian piper Patsy Touhey followed in the early 1900s. The prolific "Strathspey King" from Aberdeenshire, James Scott Skinner (1843–1927) was recorded on a Stroh violin. This instrument was specially devised to allow the bowed notes to record directly onto wax cylinder but did little to capture the tone and resonance of the fiddle. By the time the great County Sligo fiddler Michael Coleman (1891–1945) was at the height of his powers, substantial advances had been made in recording technology. His recordings, made in New York in the late 1920s, were crucial in developing the audience for this music beyond its core community. In a matter of a few years, the music of the Irish fiddle had journeyed from the dance hall to a listening audience.

Although it couldn't possibly have been known at the time, the emergence of these early recordings marked a turning point for all Celtic music and changed forever how the music was disseminated. For the first time, the music could travel out from the communities where it had been a natural, unremarkable part of life, and reach homesick exiles and musicians from other ethnic backgrounds. Most important, it could reach individuals at the heart of communities depleted by generations of emigration. Radio was the partner needed to complete this journey, and in time, Comhaltas Ceoltóirí Éireann, founded to nurture traditional music and song in Ireland, also offered a great boost to the growing interest. But more obstacles stood in the way.

Comhaltas Captures the Spirit of Ireland

Mark 1951 on your calendar of important dates in the history of Irish music. During that year, fiddlers, dancers, singers, and pipers from all across Ireland felt the stirrings of a new movement, founded by members of the Dublin Pipers' Club, to foster and generate enthusiasm for traditional music and song. Today, more than six hundred branches of Comhaltas Ceoltóirí Éireann exist worldwide and its founders' dedication to preserving Irish cultural traditions is fostered internationally.

The focus has always been on providing young people with opportunities to appreciate the traditional arts. But the movement is largely a social one in which people of all ages mix comfortably at *seisuins* (informal music sessions) and at the *fleadh cheoil* (music festivals and contests) sponsored by Comhaltas throughout Ireland and beyond. From the outset, the first annual Fleadh Cheoil na hÉireann was a huge success, and subsequent fleadhs have succeeded in drawing hundreds of musicians to compete and play at a variety of venues. The audiences for live Irish music began to grow by the thousands.

Traditional music became supremely uncool when rock and roll captured the hearts of the young folk who wanted to hear Elvis on the radio, rather than some old fogey ceilidh band. Touring showbands, covering the hits of the day, visited small towns and cities the length and breadth of Britain and

Ireland throughout the 1950s and '60s. Eventually, disco saw the showbands out of work, and all live local music struggled.

Masters and Broadcasters

Two forces at the heart of the community helped turn around the recent fortunes of traditional music. The first was a small number of teachers: key players in inspiring young people to take up the music. Dubliner Leo Rowsome (1903–1970) was an uilleann pipe maker, teacher, and piper of great renown, who held the post of Teacher of Uilleann Pipes at the Dublin College of Music from the age of nineteen. He was an inspirational player for many at a time when uilleann pipers were thin on the ground. More recently, Tom Anderson (1910–1991), the great Shetland fiddler, persuaded the local education authority to fund him to teach the fiddle in school to the young of his islands, beginning in 1977. As strong as Shetland fiddling is today, it is astonishing to consider that the music was on the wane only four decades ago. Aly Bain and Catriona Macdonald, two of today's best-known Shetland fiddlers, were both Tom Anderson's pupils, and the islands are brimming with youthful, energetic, fiddle music thanks to his efforts. It would take a lot more than rock and roll to reverse this trend now.

The second great force in the preservation and popularization of traditional music in the modern era has been radio. While live music struggled against the influx of popular music, the British Broadcasting Company (BBC) was commissioning the piper, singer, and folklorist Séamus Ennis (1919–1982) to produce *As I Roved Out*, a series of traditional music programs broadcast in the 1950s. Over a seven-year period, Ennis collected fifteen hundred field recordings from all over Ireland, Scotland, and England. This extensive archive was the first of its kind. Singer, writer, folklorist, and collector Ewan MacColl (1915–1989) produced his groundbreaking *Radio Ballads* for the BBC in the 1960s and fanned the flames of the British folk song revival in the 1960s and '70s. Alongside Ewan MacColl, with Martin Carthy, the Fisher Family, the Watersons, Donovan, and The Corries in the United Kingdom, and Ireland's Clancy Bothers, The Dubliners, and The Furey Brothers, the music was achieving a popularity never before known in folk and traditional circles. It all paved the way for the emergence of folk bands.

Seán Ó Riada's Ceoltóirí Chualann brought together the traditional elements of Irish music for the first time in a folk ensemble: fiddles, concertina, flute, uilleann pipes, and bodhrán, with Ó Riada on piano and harpsichord. The group went on to parent the earliest lineup of The Chieftains. Also emerging at this time were other influential groups featuring Andy Irvine, Mick Moloney, Paul Brady, and Donal Lunny, who helped found such seminal bands as Sweeney's Men, The Johnstons, Planxty, and the Bothy Band. Along with De Danann and Clannad, also dating from this era and still recording today, they all continue to exert a powerful influence on the music. In Scotland, Battlefield Band, The Tannahill Weavers, Silly Wizard, and Ossian were all on the ascent and offered a distinctly Scottish slant on the developing Celtic folk band sound. There was a general buzz about the music from the 1960s through the '80s that began to attract many musicians with no family or regional connection to the music. They were learning tunes and songs from records and radio broadcasts and traveling to hear authentic "source" singers and players who might read them to appreciate the genuine origins of the music. It was all beginning to blossom, and the conditions were ripening for this music to realize the levels of popularity we witness today. Needless to say, it took a couple decades for the media to pick up on this grass-roots movement.

Toward a Celtic Music

One last twist in this particular road might bring us to a clearer view on the more recent phenomenon that we know as Celtic music. From seventeenth-century Irish harper Tur-lough O'Carolan, to eighteenth-century fiddler Niel Gow, the idea that the music they were playing and composing was "Celtic" would have puzzled them. Even recently, during the rise of the earliest performing and recording folk bands of Ireland in the 1960s and '70s, none of the pre-eminent line-ups of the day would have referred to their music as anything other than "Irish" at the outset. Similarly, Scottish groups, though inspired by their Irish cousins, would largely have been playing music from Scotland, and that is how they would most likely have identified it in their early days.

Meanwhile, in Brittany, there had been a conscious effort at work to revive its traditional culture since the early part of the twentieth century. Strong ties were especially cultivated with Wales, a land with an unbroken harp tradition. Jord Cochevelou had devoted years to developing a prototype small harp, intended to revive the music of the long aban-doned Breton harp. In the hands of his nine-year-old son Alan Stivell Cochevelou, the strings of the Breton harp rang out once again in 1953, for the first time since it had graced the baronial courts of the Middle Ages four centuries earlier. Together with his father, his harp teacher Denise Megevand mixed classical works with arrangements of traditional melodies from Brittany, Ireland, Scotland, and Wales, which the young player took to immediately. He made his first recording at age eleven, and as he became more immersed in the music of the various Celtic countries, Alan Stivell broadened his instrumental base by studying at the College of Piping in Glasgow.

No doubt inspired by the growing momentum behind the music in Ireland and Scotland, Stivell soon applied his wide interest in all Celtic music to his performances and his recorded arrangements and compositions. Alan Stivell pioneered this Pan-Celtic approach more than any other artist of the time. In two concerts at the National Stadium in Dublin, November 1974, he sang of friendship between the "peasants and fishermen of Brittany and their brothers in Wales, Scotland, Ireland." His music drew upon traditions from all these places as he declared "Celtia, the meeting place of the peoples of the north and of the south, to the borders of the old world and of the new world." Electrifying performances such as these may have marked a turning point in how Irish, Scots, Welsh, and Bretons began to see their own music, appreciating its interconnectedness and potential to be developed and presented on a wider canvas. If any one person should be credited with launching the contemporary idea of an integrated "Celtic" music, it would be Alan Stivell. Certainly, his groundbreaking *Renaissance of the Celtic Harp* (1974), blending melodies from Brittany, Wales, Ireland, Scotland, and the Isle of Man, is today regarded as having realized the very goal of its title. (See Chapter 6: "The Music" and Chapteer 7: "Celtic Music on CD.") It sparked a worldwide fascination with Celtic music for the small harp and inspired more people to learn the instrument than at any time in history.

All this is only to suggest one road map that may have led Celtic music on its journey to present day prominence. There is still a detailed atlas to be explored. Turn its pages and you might map the route of fiddle players from Orkney who went to work for the Hudson Bay company in the nineteenth century. They passed their tunes and dances along to native Athabaskan fiddlers in Alaska, who still uphold their traditions with great pride. Or you might detour via Newfoundland and stop at the map followed by Irish-speaking fishery workers, who named the town of St. John's after a parish in Waterford and left an indelible imprint on the music of the Canadian province. Then follow to North Carolina the Hebridean Scots, whose charismatic Gaelic psalm singing had a direct influence on the African American Baptist music of today's American South. The maps of the British Isles and Ireland alone would show a trading of people and a mixing and mingling of influences among all the home nations across all time. And all along the way, singers have been singing their ballads, and dancers birling to the sound of fiddle and pipes far removed from the business of developing a performance art or selling units of music.

As an abbreviated map only, ours doesn't begin to cover the unique stories of musical resurgence in all the Celtic nations and regions. Other contributions to the big picture will be touched upon in later chapters. What this story does offer is an insight into an inspirational, tenacious musical spirit, typically Celtic, holding fast against tidal waves of change and adversity.

The next chapter of the story will likely see the music flowing farther outward from its sources and deeper into the world's great musical ocean. Celtic traveling musicians have been importing ideas for generations, and the urge to reach out and exchange seems stronger than ever. In the 1960s, Andy Irvine's travels in the Balkans brought exciting new rhythms and instruments into Irish music. In more recent years, Capercaillie and Martyn Bennett, Scottish musicians with deep roots in Scots Gaelic instrumental music and song, have embraced a Celtic/Afro/Caribbean blend. Others are finding inspiration in Latin rhythms and arrangements: John Whelan, MacUmba, Eileen Ivers. They all manage to avoid drowning in a generic ethnic musical soup by striking the crucial balance between root and branch, tradition and innovation, and this has to be the goal at the more experimental edge of the music. Meanwhile, traditional fiddle, pipe, and harp teachers are in full demand, step-dancing classes are oversubscribed, tickets for hot ceilidh bands sell out within days, and in the last decade, Glasgow's Celtic Connections has grown into the biggest winter music festival in the world. The widespread availability of recordings is generating new international audiences and digital/computer home recording and duplication technology is giving musicians unprecedented control in the packaging and distribution of their music. It may be the first time in history that we can confidently predict the story of Celtic music will be never-ending.

THREE

Varieties of Celtic Music

For the people of the Celtic countries and regions, heritage is not a cultural theme park. It is an aspect of everyday life, whether consciously experienced or not. A song, a story, a turn of phrase, a spoken accent, a game, a dance, a craft: Each generation learns these anew, reinterprets them in their own place and time, and passes them along. While the music clearly comes from a variety of distinct sources, some of it transcends its wide geography, especially the more hybrid, contemporary forms. But much of the authentic traditional music is place-specific.

It was originally an academic classification along linguistic lines that saw Celtic places organized as follows: Speakers of Irish, Scottish Gaelic, and Manx, the native tongue of the Isle of Man, were referred to as Goidelic or Q-Celtic, so called because they preserved the Indo-European "qu" in their speech. In Welsh, Cornish, and Breton speakers, this was transformed into "p," and their language became known as Brythonic or

P-Celtic. These distinctions also follow the geography of the Atlantic Celts and so offer a convenient organizational aid in this chapter. Galicia and Asturias on the Spanish coastline, which lost its Celtic language, are included as a natural cultural extension after Brittany in France. And from that southern point, westward across the Atlantic bridge to the New World, the Celtic-rooted music of Scottish Canadians, Irish Americans, and the Southern Appalachians are all included here.

The Old World

Ireland Arthur O' Shaughnessy famously described the Irish as "the music makers" and "the dreamers of dreams." To suggest that they have channeled their hopes, dreams, and national spirit through their country's music is possibly an understatement.

Everything we have considered so far, and the varieties of music to be examined in this chapter, reinforce the fact that there is no one way to pin down this music. It is certainly the case with the musical traditions of Ireland. At times, these have struggled to survive in a country ravaged by continuous invasion, dating back to the Danes who were repelled by King Brian Boru in the eleventh century. The Normans, arriving in 1169, found a bardic tradition already well established, and they embraced and patronized these early medieval musicians and mostly assimilated with the native Gaels. Normans imported the poetic customs of the French and Spanish courts evolving into traditional Irish love songs or *amhrán*.

As was discussed earlier in Chapter 2, "The Story of Celtic Music," waves of English invasions from the fifteenth century onward ravaged the bardic way of life and its musical legacy. Eventually, the Great Famine of the nineteenth century and its aftermath had as deeply a destructive effect upon the natural cycles and regional geography of the music. Yet it has endured and enjoyed a phenomenal revival within Ireland, and it has sprouted everywhere Irish immigrants arrived to plant new roots.

Caoineadh, or laments, are the oldest song style surviving in Irish music, including *keening,* a form of lamenting at a funeral. Other laments document tragedies and are sung in the style of *sean nós.* Literally "old style," this is a highly ornamented form of unaccompanied singing in which notes are varied, stretched, stopped, and decorated (see Chapter 4, "Celtic Music Deconstructed").

A strong melodic line, ornamented heavily, may also describe Irish instrumental music. Traditional musicians impress their individual or regionally acquired technique upon the melody, using slides, grace notes, and other masterful techniques. Although harp and pipe airs may date back much farther, the majority of tunes played today in Ireland are dances, such as jigs, reels, hornpipes, slides, and polkas, written at some point in the last three centuries.

The defining instruments of Irish instrumental music are harp, uilleann pipes, fiddle, flute, whistle, and button accordion. String instruments such as banjo, mandolin, and bouzouki have had an escalating influence on the sound through the twentieth century until the present day. These traditional instruments have been combined with new musical innovations and ideas ever since Irish folk bands first came to prominence in the 1970s. Their musical approach was highly influential throughout all Celtic music at that time, and the revival of interest in Irish traditions is an inspirational force sweeping through Scotland to Wales, Brittany, and on to the United States.

Irish Melodies, Scottish Airs

During the nineteenth century, one and a half million copies of the sheet music for "The Last Rose of Summer" were sold in the United States alone. It is one of the most popular songs ever written. Its composer, Thomas Moore (1779–1852), was an Irish poet, musician, singer, and writer and Ireland's first internationally celebrated man of letters. Through his work, he gave his contemporary countrymen and -women a deeper understanding of their cultural heritage during their struggle for freedom. That he did all this while soaring to heights of fame as a pillar of British romanticism, along with Sir Walter Scott and Lord Byron, was remarkable even then. It was, however, the main reason for Moore becoming unfashionable even by the end of his own lifetime. Today, Moore is rarely heard in Ireland, his music viewed with suspicion as having been crafted for eighteenth-century Anglo-Irish drawing rooms.

Moore lived at a volatile and divided period in Irish history. During his lifetime, Ireland was integrated politically and economically into Great Britain, with little regard for the rights, let alone the cultural life of its people. Moore pursued his career on the shores of England and was feted by the establishment there, even though he espoused radical views and worked to generate sympathy for the Irish cause. Drawing upon Ireland's cultural heritage, its mythology, and its music, Moore shaped traditional material into art songs modeled after the *amhran* of the ancient bardic tradition. His work set the stage for Ireland's literary and dramatic movement led by William Butler Yeats in the early twentieth century.

James Flannery, the noted author and singer, has set the work of Moore in a new and sympathetic light by placing it in the context of his day, and of ancient times to present. In his landmark book and CD collection *Dear Harp of My Country,* he notes that Moore was creating his work at a complicated time in Irish history, attempting to fuse the ancient bardic order with the sophisticated art songs appropriate to his time. As Ireland's political landscape moved and shifted in the generations ahead, Moore's work became associated with the dying freedoms of his age, rather than being lifted through time as part of the story of Irish identity and struggle.

Like Scotland's Robert Burns, Thomas Moore was chiefly a writer of lyrics, which he would then set to traditional airs (many of which were lifted directly from Edward Bunting's *General Collection of the Ancient Music of Ireland*). However, Burns wrote at a time in Scotland when the tumultuous events of his country's union with England had already taken place earlier in the eighteenth century. In gaining political stability, Scots had courted a crisis of cultural identity, which the work of Burns helped to heal. He enabled Scots keep in touch with their roots through the folk melodies of their land. And so it has been since.

The work of Burns as collector and preserver of traditional airs and song fragments no doubt inspired Thomas Moore. However, living in England during a turbulent time in Anglo-Irish history, Moore could not always speak his mind. The messages of his songs often were disguised by allusions expressed in the flowery poetry of the time. The Irish and Scottish attitudes toward their two poets makes a vivid contrast even today.

Scotland A quick helicopter tour of Scotland would highlight its physical diversity. An audio tour would deliver a powerful message of innovation and variety in the traditional arts, particularly among the young. The traditional music scene throughout Scotland has never been healthier.

Although the most widely disseminated images of Scotland are of majestic hillsides and wild moorlands, 80 percent of the population lives and works in the urban Central Belt, between the rivers of the Clyde and the Forth. City-dwelling instrumentalists and song-makers from Glasgow, Falkirk, Edinburgh, Dundee, and Aberdeen have always made an enormous contribution to the nation's musical life. More than that, it is the sheer diversity of landscape and lifestyle that echoes through the music, and which can never be represented by any one style, instrument, or voice.

It shouldn't be assumed that the proximity to England dilutes the character of the Scottish Borders. On the contrary, Scots is spoken widely there, and the disputes over the lie of the very border itself, along with other family territorial quarrels, gave rise to the great body of song known as the "Border Ballads."

For centuries, the Borderlands between Scotland and England were wild and lawless. There was constant feuding, robbery, and cattle theft by *reivers*, or raiders, among the family groups of the area, regardless of whether they lived north or south of the border. These violent times gave rise to a great ballad tradition, celebrating the outlaws and lamenting the strife of border warfare. Anyone who had the pleasure of hearing border shepherd Willie Scott deliver one of these epics would have been left in no doubt of the strength of the region's character.

The Mother Tongue

Scotland has three native tongues: English; Gaelic, an Indo-European language related to Irish; and Scots, a dialect blending expressions from old English, French, Gaelic, and Norse, with indigenous words. Emerging almost a thousand years ago, many people feel that Scots is such a rich mode of expression, it should be considered a distinct language, rather than a dialect of English.

On a visit to Edinburgh, you might be forgiven for thinking that Scots, as a living language, has died out. Stroll a mile or so from the cosmopolitan city center into the port of Leith, or cross the Forth Bridge into the Kingdom of Fife, and you'll easily convince yourself to the contrary. Whether the *lallans* of the Lowlands or the *doric* of the Northeast, Scots is alive and well in many parts of the country. Its lack of status meant it never suffered legislated persecution endured by Gaelic in the bad old days. But neither has it enjoyed very much in the way of formal support, unlike Gaelic today. Nevertheless, many songs and poetry written in Scots continue to develop "the mither tongue" and build upon a written Scots heritage dating back to medieval times. The work of songwriters like Karine Polwart and Davy Steele will, in time, find their own place in the tradition.

Travel northward to the Central Belt, and you will notice that language and landscape change quickly. In the intense urban landscape of Glasgow, a unique culture and character is palpable. It is deeply rooted and very contemporary, most obvious in Glaswegians' celebrated sense of humor and their pride in creations such as the progressive Celtic music festival, Celtic Connections. There is grit and substance in Glasgow songs, where traditional industries such as shipbuilding, once the "Pride of the Clyde," tell of a bygone age. Comedian, television broadcaster, and movie actor Billy Connolly drifted from work in the shipyards on the River Clyde into a folksinger's life as a member of the Humblebums, with Gerry Rafferty, who had an international hit with "Baker Street" in the 1980s. Billy Connolly has since taken Glasgow humor and patter or banter to the world and has a wealth of anecdotes on the folk scene in 1960s and '70s Scotland.

Edinburgh, which annually plays host to the world's largest International Arts Festival, is also home today to a thriving ceilidh culture. Musicians from far afield travel to the capital to become involved in the city's pub session scene, invigorated by the likes of concertina virtuoso Simon Thoumire and traditional trio Fine Friday. In the 1980s, the members of The Easy Club came together in the city. Inspired by Duke Ellington's comment that only two types of music swing—jazz and Scottish music—they created a gutsy, rhythmic instrumental style that bridged the gap between traditional music and jazz. Their influence was felt in Ireland and beyond, and their style is now associated particularly with the Edinburgh scene. The voice of Dick Gaughan, meanwhile, is the sound of Edinburgh's—and Scotland's—working man. Raised by the Leith docklands, he combines grit and sensitivity, anger and compassion in his interpretations of traditional and original material.

Another city with a mighty musical identity is Dundee. Its history of seafaring generated whaling songs in the nineteenth century, and earlier songs of the sea told often of life in exotic climes, or of young women disguising themselves as boys and running away to sea to be reunited with sailor boyfriends. After a visit to the port city, Robert Burns spoke out on an eighteenth-century disgrace that attracted comment this early from too few other writers.

The poet was moved by the sight of a slave ship in the harbor en route from Senegal to Virginia. With his keen ear for melody, Burns had picked up a Spanish Sephardic tune *Rachel's Lamentation for Her Children* from another Scots collector's tome, *The Roxburgh Ballads.* Perhaps believing the melody was also known in Moorish North Africa, he used it as the setting for verses pronouncing his abhorrence of slavery in "The Slaves' Lament."

Jute was imported into the port from India and woven into sails, covered wagon tops for the pioneers of the American

West, and eventually sandbags for the trenches of World War I. The toil of Dundee's jute mill workers was a breeding ground for music and song into the twentieth century. Women were the mainstay of the mills, and today Dundee is still known for its strong tradition of women ballad singers such as Maureen Jelks and Sheena Wellington. Their repertoires reveal the social history of Dundee's mill workers' communities and reinforce the tradition of work songs in Scotland, unparalleled in all of Celtic music.

Beyond the fishing port and North Sea oil center of Aberdeen, the Northeast is farming country, a great repository of *muckle sangs,* or big ballads, and of descriptions of farm life vividly re-created in the *bothy ballads*. Unmarried men would gather at *feeing fairs,* or hiring markets, and contract to work on particular farms for the coming season. In rich language and bawdy humor, they would go on to describe their experiences and include warnings against especially hard conditions on some of the farms. The laborers lived in small huts, or *bothies,* where they gathered to share company and songs in the evenings. Their bothy ballads are still sung by many of today's Scots musicians.

Agricultural ways, once a lifestyle for thousands, are well documented in countless traditional songs sung in the rich Scots tongue of Doric. Aberdeen was also home to one of the last century's greatest ballad singers, Jeannie Robertson, whom American folklorist Alan Lomax called "a monumental figure of world folksong." Her ancestors belonged to two of the long-established families of Travelers, the Robertsons and the Stewarts, itinerant workers who roamed the Northeast and beyond. Their reputation as musicians, singers, and storytellers lives on today (see Chapter 4, "Celtic Music Deconstructed"). Jeannie Robertson's prowess as an interpreter of the great ballads was legendary, and she was held to be a spellbinding performer.

The Northeast is also celebrated for its fiddle music, especially Victorian fiddle master James Scott Skinner (1843–1927). Along with the Central Highlands of Perthshire, the fiddle music of this region is held to be among the oldest in the country. The bowing style of the Northeast has a particular emphasis on a quick snap on the upstroke of the bow—the Scots snap—and is the most dominant force in today's Scots fiddle music.

The Northern Isles—Orkney and Shetland—have strong cultural links with Scandinavia, having been part of Scotland for a mere four centuries. This is echoed in the islanders' speech and especially in their fiddle music, for which Shetlanders, such as Aly Bain and Catriona Macdonald, both pupils of the inspirational teacher Tom Anderson, are particularly famed.

Westward of the Scottish mainland is the Hebrides. Along with the Western Highlands on the Scottish mainland, this is the traditional homeland of the Gaels. From as far back as the twelfth century, this society was governed by a clan system, where the clan chief was responsible for the welfare of his extended family. Music, poetry, and storytelling were all greatly valued, and clan chiefs would retain a piper, harper, and bard. This way of life collapsed after the Battle of Culloden in 1746. It was further decimated by mass migration in the centuries since, but to this day, the sense of musical heritage remains strong in the Highlands and Islands of Scotland through the work of traditional Gaelic singers and song-based groups. Gaelic song traditions seize the imagination of nonspeakers in Scotland and beyond. Especially fascinating are the *waulking songs,* rhythmic Hebridean weavers' work songs, sung to lighten and coordinate the work of "waulking," or shrinking tweed cloth. Waulkings became social occasions in which groups of women pounded and passed wet, woven cloth around a table for hours until it was fully shrunk. These were call-and-response songs, sometimes with rude lyrics, and they would have helped to take the monotony out of the hard labor. Waulking songs traveled to Cape Breton, where they became known as *milling songs*. Mouth music, or *puirt-a-beul,* is another riveting Gaelic singing technique, developed to mimic instrumental sounds, especially bagpipes, and dance rhythms (see Chapter 4, "Celtic Music Deconstructed").

In 1981, traditional musicians and singers on the Island of Barra decided to arouse interest in the traditional arts by setting up a summer school on the island, with tutors from across Scotland invited to provide Gaelic song and instrumental instruction to young islanders. It was the beginning of the *Feisean* movement, now common throughout the Highlands and Islands of Scotland and still gathering momentum. Each *feis* varies in its emphasis, and countless young people have benefited in these largely residential programs.

Voice of the Gael

Unfortunately, Scotland compares poorly with Ireland, Wales, and Brittany in responding to the threat to the survival of its ancient native Celtic language. Completely distinct from the hybrid tongue of Scots, Scottish Gaelic is a Goidelic or Q-Celtic language related to Irish, and its speakers suffered tremendous intolerance for centuries. Until recent decades, the use of Gaelic at school was not encouraged even among native speakers. As a result Gaelic is the mother tongue of less than 2 percent of Scots today, whereas Breton is still spoken as the first language of 16 percent of the population of Brittany. Thankfully, the urge to save Gaelic is now felt across Scotland. According to a recent poll, 66 percent of all Scots strongly believe that the language should be preserved and promoted as a matter of urgency. Today, the nationwide movement to revitalize Gaelic has significant momentum behind it, with immersion courses in the language being taught even from nursery level.

Most native speakers live in the western Highlands and especially in the islands of the Inner and Outer Hebrides, scattered in the Atlantic off the northwestern Scottish mainland. Beginning in the 1950s, Flora MacNeil of the Island of Barra was one of the first singers of unaccompanied Gaelic song to take this heritage of music, poetry, and stories to a non-Gaelic-speaking audience. Along with her daughter Maggie MacInnes, she still continues this legacy. Since the 1970s and '80s, the music of bands like Runrig and Capercaillie has been of particular importance in reclaiming this ancient language and sharing its cultural heritage with an international audience.

Finally, the southwest region of Scotland is powerfully associated with the life and work of Robert Burns. Few individuals have done as much to preserve the song heritage of Scotland than the man rightly known as the National Bard. His collected volumes of verse are more popular today than ever.

From the rolling hills of The Borders, to the fishing villages of the East Coast, the Atlantic islands of the West, and the Norse seasoned Northeast, Scotland's natural heritage appears to provide the perfect landscape for inspiring its indigenous music. Modern travel and communication connections mean more musicians from the Highlands and Islands to the Lowlands can live and work in the landscape that most inspires. They are celebrating their roots by preserving traditional styles, and crafting new songs that speak for a very contemporary Scotland.

The Isle of Man The very name of the Isle of Man stirs the imagination, with its roots in the mythology of the Celtic god of the sea, Manannan Mac Lir. Its position in the Irish Sea between Ireland and England caused the island to be buffeted by many influences through the centuries. It has been governed by the Scots and the English and was invaded by the Norse. Linguistic influences from all these places mingled in the native Manx language, although from the fourth century onward, an Irish and Scots influenced Gaelic tongue was the predominant speech heard on the island. In 1866, the Isle of Man gained home rule, but even so, the Manx language began to decline in the second half of the nineteenth century. English became increasingly common in recent generations, and the last native speaker of Manx died in 1974. A linguistic revival is under way these days, however, and Manx language street signs are now seen in Douglas, the capital town, and beyond.

Awareness of Celtic music is so dependent today on the availability of recordings. Only a few artists have taken Manx music out to the world, notably harper Charles Guard and harper and singer Emma Christian. For this reason Manx musical traditions have a low profile. Song traditions were always strong there, covering seafaring tales, work songs, ballads, and lullabies. Unfortunately, as in Wales, the Methodist Church had an oppressive effect on traditional singing, music, and dance, and by the mid-twentieth century, religious songs had replaced almost all forms of traditional music. Islanders already had a body of sacred songs of which the Manx carols *Carvalyn Gailckagh* are the best-known examples, and with church approval, these became even more popular.

The spark of interest that ignited the linguistic revival spread to traditions in music and dance in the late twentieth century. Although the language may never again be widely spoken on the island, Manx ceilidhs and Scottish-style feisean are easily imaginable.

Wales When the British Celts had traveled as far west as they could in retreat from invading Angles and Saxons, they settled in the hilly country they called Cymru, the land of comrades. The peace was never lasting, and there were many battles between the English and the people the Anglo-Saxons called the *weahlas,* or foreigners. Although Henry VIII passed an act annexing Wales under English rule and tried to suppress the Welsh language, the culture endured.

Welsh music is today characterized by a strong vocal tradition, most celebrated in the Welsh choirs of former coal-mining communities. Sacred songs and harmony are an important part of the tradition, which also features the unique and ancient form of *pennillion,* where a singer performs alongside a harper although each follows a different melody.

For well over a thousand years, Wales has upheld an unbroken heritage of harp playing, and it remains a pillar of the music. Uniquely in Celtic music, Welsh players traditionally play the triple harp, which came into the country from Italy in the seventeenth century. It is larger than other Celtic harps, with three rows of strings. The two outside rows are equivalent to the white notes on a piano keyboard, and the inside row sustains the black chromatic notes. The music has been passed down to today's leading triple harper, Robin Huw Bowen, from direct performance, itinerant musicians, manuscripts, and, more recently, the highly influential teacher Nancy Richards and her pupils such as Llio Rhydderch.

Apart from the strength of the Welsh harp traditions, the

music in general has struggled in the face of social and religious revolution, and the numbing effects of striving for Victorian respectability. The Methodist movement took hold in Wales in the late eighteenth and nineteenth century, and devout Methodists frowned upon all forms of dance, harp playing, and fiddling. Some harpers burned their instruments during this time or concealed them under their beds for long periods. Although the harp survived, other Welsh instrumental traditions, such as the Welsh fiddle, have struggled ever since. Thanks to the efforts of pioneering bands such as Ar Log, 4 Yn Y Bar, Mabsant, Cilmeri, Plethyn, and Crasdant, this situation has improved in the last three decades. The music of the pibcorn, or hornpipe, has also seen a recent revival. This primitive reed instrument has a wooden chanter attached to a piece of naturally curving cow's horn. Like the Breton bombarde, its sound is extremely powerful.

With a recently established Welsh assembly, there is a sense that the future development of Welsh traditional music and culture is at last in the right hands. Triple harper Robin Huw Bowen feels strongly about this. According to Bowen, "Wales never really seemed to feature much in the world of Celtic music when I first touched on it. Many people in fact would have said that Wales never had any such folk music, or if it had existed, it had all been lost. . . . It was no surprise that young Welsh people (including myself) who were interested in real folk music would turn towards Gaelic and Breton sources, rather than those of their own country. By now of course, things are different, and Welsh traditional music in its true form is making a comeback. We know that it's not Irish music, nor Breton or Scottish, but our tradition is just as valid and unique and should be considered as much a part of Celtic culture as all the rest."

The Bardic Tradition: Eisteddfodau

In 1176, according to a manuscript from the time, Lord Rys ap Gruffudd held a seated gathering, an *eisteddfod,* at his castle in Cardigan, Wales. A twelfth-century patron of the arts, he invited poets and musicians from all over the country and awarded the best poet and musician a chair at his head table. In the years that followed, many *eisteddfodau* were held throughout Wales under the patronage of Welsh gentry and noblemen. Today, an *eisteddfod* is a series of music and poetry competitions, and hundreds of small local and school *eisteddfodau* are held throughout Wales all year round. It is a particular tradition that St. David's Day (Dydd Gwyl Dewi Sant on March 1st) be celebrated with an *eisteddfod,* especially in Welsh schools.

On a national level, 1880 saw the formation of an association to ensure that a grand-scale music festival, based around the traditions of ancient Welsh bardic competition, was staged every year. With the exception of the war years of 1914 and 1940, The Royal National Eisteddfod, Yr Eisteddfod Genedlacthol, has succeeded in reaching this impressive goal.

The main festival takes place on a different site each year, to ensure that it visits every part of the country. In keeping with tradition, the most prestigious competition at "the National" is still poetry based, with the main award being the Chair, a specially commissioned piece of fine furniture that harks back to the days of the first bardic gatherings in ancient courts. The prize for poetry in "free meters" (not following the traditional poetic pattern) is a crown, and it is considered a great honor to win either prize. Indeed, prizes are only awarded when the entries are deemed to have reached the high standard set by previous years' winners. The ceremonies for the chairing and the crowning of the bards are filled with tradition and color. The winners are escorted from the audience to the stage to receive their prizes amidst a pageant of dancing flower girls and great applause. At the Wales

International ceremony, expatriates from all over the world join in the festivities.

Many traditional Welsh musicians have criticized the Eisteddfod organization for stifling true Welsh traditions in favor of a classical approach to Welsh music. They also maintain that the competitive atmosphere inhibits young people from embracing traditional music in a natural, informal atmosphere. In response, the Eisteddfod has attempted to cater for more progressive tastes by staging Welsh rock bands. It has also grown to include competitions in crafts, dancing, folk singing, choral, drama, theater, and many other arts. But the festival will always be associated with a more classical interpretation of Welsh culture: Famous Welsh singers who began their careers at "the National" include Sir Geraint Evans and the internationally renowned bass baritone Bryn Terfel. He has performed there with the BBC National Orchestra of Wales, offering new Welsh works by Pwyll ap Sion and Iwan Llwyd. Meanwhile, keeping traditions in Welsh music alive at the Eisteddfod in recent years have been singer songwriter Dafydd Iwan and also Ar Log, the first band from Wales to record traditional Welsh song and dance in 1978.

Cornwall The peninsular Duchy of Cornwall sits at the extreme Southwest of England, pointing like a toe out into the Atlantic. Like all the Celtic countries and regions, its character is formed by the sea, by rocky coastlines, by mythology such as the Arthurian legend of the Lost Land of Lyonesse, and by isolation from the land-based movements of people across Europe. Cornwall was always reached by sea.

Cornwall came under English rule in the tenth century, and by the mid-sixteenth century, the Cornish language was officially sidelined. The last native speakers, for whom Cornish was their only language, had died out by the mid-seventeenth century, but pockets of speech and Cornish dialect endured in the most remote corners of the land. The Cornish have shown themselves to be just as keen as the Manx to resurrect their language in recent years. And like the Manx, they uphold a strong tradition of carol singing, with different carols associated with different towns and regions in the Duchy.

The Methodists did their best to save the Cornish from the sin of traditional music, as they had done with the Welsh and the Manx. However, the loss of the language was probably even more damaging to traditional Cornish music, especially song, which mostly vanished. Fiddles were common in the fishing communities, and Cornish ceilidhs or *troyll* are still remembered by the older fisherfolk today. Like their Welsh neighbors, some of these villages had male-voice choirs, and some continue to perform. Nowadays, Cornish coastal towns are popular retirement destinations and artist communities with a robust tourist industry. This has tended to undermine many of the older community-based music traditions. On the other hand, local groups like Bucca and Dalla have revitalized many of the old Cornish tunes and playing styles, and the popularity of the annual Cornish Gorsedd cultural festival, along with the Cornish language classes, suggests that Cornwall remains a proud and independent land with a Celtic soul.

Brittany About 1,500 years ago, British Celts voyaged southward across the sea and invaded Armorica, now Brittany in Western France. Brittany (Little Britain) merged with France in 1532 when a treaty was signed that gave the French kings sovereignty. By the late eighteenth century, the region was formerly absorbed into France, and by the nineteenth century, Bretons were actively involved in working to preserve their Celtic language and cultural heritage.

The people of Brittany love their music and, above all, they love dance music. Propelled in human chains and circles by singers and musicians, they will often tirelessly generate song after tune until dawn. Bretons demonstrate their love of music and dance at *festou noz*, or night festivals. These occasions differ from Scottish and Irish ceilidhs in two important ways: They are held in the open-air in the summertime, and the Breton equivalent of the Irish ceilidh band doesn't usually play for the dancers. Instead, the music is often provided by *couples de sonneurs*, pairs of singers and pipers, who alternate duties through the night. Because their job is to supply energetic and regulated dance tunes, they don't sing duets leading into old Breton sing-alongs. Stamina is the quality they cultivate. Their singing style is known as *kan ha diskan*, or chant and counterchant, where singers trade the melody of the song back and forth with a characteristic overlap at the end of each phrase. The singing progresses steadily, holding fast to the rhythm of the dance, in a pattern identical to that followed by the pipers. They also perform in pairs with one playing a small bagpipe, or *binou*, and the other a high-pitched oboe-like instrument called the *bombarde*.

With *gavotten, dans plinn, an dros, fisels, ronds*—in all more than twenty-five different types of dances—music makers at a *fest noz* can be kept busy all night long. Singers and pipers will offer a variety of rhythms for the dancers at most *festou noz*, while, in the more traditional gatherings, they'll perform exclusively the melodies suited to the local dance of the region. The intricate steps and rhythms that characterize each dance vary from village to village, so it becomes easy to identify the stranger in town!

Dances, and the tunes that accompany them, date back centuries in Brittany, which is why it's surprising to learn that the first public *festou noz* were organized in 1955 and 1957.

The late 1940s saw the formation of the first Breton pipe bands, notably the celebrated Bagad Kemper in 1949. In the mid-1950s, a resurrection of Breton harp playing by Alan Stivell and a renewed and growing interest in kan ha diskan reunited many Bretons with remarkable aspects of their culture they may have forgotten. Multi-instrumental groups such as Kornog, Sonerien Du, Tammles, and Skolvan featured accordion, guitar, flute, and fiddle, with indigenous instruments as well. Their contemporary sound extended the range of traditional singers, bombarde, and binou players. The international profile of Stivell and guitarist Dan Ar Braz helped Breton music to reach a new audience both at home and throughout the world. Their new compositions fall into step alongside traditional tunes and songs, including the ballads, or *gwerz,* sung unaccompanied. Today Breton is the most spoken of all the Celtic languages, and its speakers foresee a future for their music as surely healthy as it will be melodic.

Galicia and Asturias It is no accident that each of the Celtic countries and regions hugs miles of coastline. Proximity to the sea sits at the very core of their identity, and the sea sustained their connections in the days when ocean routes were the main means of travel and trade.

Celtic tribes had migrated into northern Spain in the Bronze Age, and these settlers, known by the Romans as the Gallaecia, gave the region its name. About 1,500 years ago, British Celts voyaged southward and invaded Brittany in Western France. These groups continued farther southward along the coastline and, along with the Irish, had ongoing contact with the people in Galicia and Asturias, sharing music and cultural beliefs. No Celtic language remains from this era; however, some words from Celtic roots are scattered through the Galician Romance language of Gallego.

The Shrine of Saint James at Compostela meant that Galicia was a destination for Christian pilgrims in medieval times. Santiago de Compostela became a center of learning and culture, and the collection of four hundred *Cantigas de Santa Maria* (songs for the Virgin Mary) were developed there. Although they are considered an invaluable element in Spanish medieval music, the *Cantigas* also bring to light Galicia's Celtic heritage. Several of the *Cantiga* stories are located in Britain and feature the sagas of Celtic seafarers, warriors, and even characters from Welsh Arthurian legends.

The harp and bagpipes echo through this Spanish Celtic corner. The Galician pipes, or *gaita,* have been shared with international audiences through the recordings and performances of Carlos Núñez. Along with the multi-instrumental lineup of Milladoiro and Susana Seivane, he has introduced many to the Celtic connection with the Spanish Iberian peninsula.

The New World

Irish Americans Earlier chapters have sketched some of the story of Irish emigration—the flight from persecution and famine and the growing settlements in U.S. cities of the East Coast and Midwest (see Chapter 2, "The Story of Celtic Music"). By the middle of the nineteenth century, a quarter of the populations of New York and Chicago were native Irish.

During the American Civil War, Irish immigrants were drafted into both armies, with most of those in the Union Irish Brigade volunteering. A total of 150,000 men lost their lives in the conflict. In post–Civil War years, the urban communities burgeoned with industry, attracting more workers from throughout the world. Demand for entertainment of all sorts grew, and Irish musicians, singers, and comedians found they had a role to play. By the time the Vaudeville era emerged, the theater was providing work for thousands of Irish variety entertainers, but the cities were also great hubs of traditional music, with pipers' clubs and Gaelic Leagues popular coast to coast. So although Irish American music has seen something of a golden age in recent decades, it has really been at the hub of urban life in the United States since the first Irish men and women disembarked at city quays.

Nowadays, with the ease of international travel, many first-, second-, and third-generation Irish can share in the cultural life of Ireland and the United States. The influence of Irish immigrant and home-based fiddlers, pipers, and flute players of the 1920s through to the present time can be heard in the performances of many of today's Irish American musicians. The parents of Chicago fiddler Liz Carroll were born in Ireland, and she finds the connection to both countries a great source of strength and, sometimes, confusion: "You don't quite belong in America and you don't quite belong in Ireland. I would imagine that it's the same for those people in England whose parents or grandparents come from Ireland."

Only in recent years have Irish American musicians and singers felt comfortable experimenting with tradition. Previously, in striving to make their music sound as authentic as possible, they would eschew any influences from the great interwoven fabric of American music surrounding them. Having heard musicians in Ireland occasionally having fun with bluegrass runs or rock riffs, some realized that, growing up in America, they were best placed to show where Irish music sits in a wider spectrum. No matter how dedicated they are to seeking out Irish traditional musical communities, realistically they are more likely to hear every other type of music in their neighborhoods and via media outlets. Fiddler Martin

Hayes and button accordion player John Whelan, who have settled in the United States, along with first-generation Irish-American Bronx fiddler Eileen Ivers, have all led the way in allowing Irish musical traditions to inhale the multicultural atmosphere of American music. Latin, Afro Caribbean, rock, and jazz rhythms pulse around their strong Irish melody lines. Along with contributing enthusiasm and support for traditional music in Ireland, Irish Americans are also finally celebrating their New World roots.

Emigrant ships carried songs, poems, and stories as well as people in their holds. Many traditional songs speak eloquently of the plight of immigrants and give us intimate insights into the lives of those who left and the forces that propelled them. They go beyond statistics and historical documents, measuring the scale of emigration from Ireland. They speak for all the voices passing them on in an unbroken line from singer to singer, and this gets to the heart and soul of their beauty. Today, more than forty-four million Americans claim Irish ancestry. A steady exodus continues today— more than five hundred each week— which tells us why Irish emigration songs are still being written.

Scottish Canadians In Chapter 2, "The Story of Celtic Music," we followed the fate of Highland Scots, forcibly cleared from their smallholdings in the nineteenth century. The settlers that lined up to replace them were sheep, all part of landowners' plans to increase the profit margin on their lands. In the years to come, the Clearances and their aftermath saw a fairly densely populated landscape empty across the Highlands and Islands, as thousands followed the evicted communities to the Lowlands, England, Australia, New Zealand, the United States, and Canada.

Cape Breton Island, Nova Scotia, received thirty thousand

cleared Highlanders in the nineteenth century. They joined a community of some twenty thousand Scottish Gaels who had emigrated there several decades earlier, bringing their Gaelic language and songs, their dances, and their fiddle and pipe music. By the beginning of the twentieth century, there were around eighty to ninety thousand Gaelic speakers in Cape Breton. They were remote, sheltered from the influences of most other cultures, and they were able to preserve an old fiddle style and much of their Gaelic song. Cape Breton's very isolation, allied with the Gaels' natural love of their language and culture, allowed the islanders to maintain, across two centuries, a continuous tradition of Highland fiddling from a golden age of Scottish music. Gaelic waulking songs, sung by tweed weavers in the Hebrides, were preserved in Cape Breton as milling songs. Step dancing thrived there as it all but fell into distant memory in Scotland. Today Cape Breton Island stands as the only remaining center of Scottish Gaelic language and culture in North America, and as confirmation of the tenacity of oral tradition.

Mary Jane Lamond's formative years were spent moving between Quebec and Ontario, but she soaked up her Gaelic heritage over many summers visiting her grandparents in Cape Breton. It was there that she first remembers hearing Gaelic songs. Her initiation took place at a milling frolic, a re-created Hebridean waulking where a heavy woolen cloth is repeatedly beaten against a table and people gather to sing and keep time to the rhythm of the work. The potency of that experience and the singing she heard captured Lamond's imagination. Her recordings of Gaelic songs show her love of the tradition and her interest in exploring its boundaries within contemporary music. And like many fellow Cape Bretoners, she is determined to preserve the Gaelic heritage of her home, just as fiddlers Buddy and Natalie MacMaster have done so much to spread the rhythmic, driving fiddle traditions of Cape Breton, never separating them from the dance. Older piping styles also predominate on the island, allied to the fiddle and dance styles, compelling Scottish pipers such as Hamish and Fin Moore to bring the raw energy of Cape Breton music back home.

The Southern Appalachians Many Southerners identify themselves as "Scotch Irish." But who are they exactly? In the early 1600s, James I of England (and VI of Scotland) earmarked Protestant tenant farmers in the Scottish Lowlands to colonize the north of Ireland. In a ten-year period, eight thousand took the opportunity to escape poor harvests and the feudal arrangements of Scottish land occupancy, settling in Ulster. From 1690 to 1715, more than fifty thousand Presbyterian Scots joined them, and their migration had a permanent effect upon the character and history of Ulster. The year 1717 saw the first wave of these "Ulster Scots" emigrate farther west to the United States to escape rent war and religious persecution. Between 1717 and the Revolutionary War, more than a quarter of a million Ulster Scots made the crossing and settled along the Eastern slopes of the Appalachians.

Scottish Gaels, exiled both as a result of the final failure of the Jacobite risings in 1746 and Highland Clearance deportations, sailed up the Cape Fear River in eastern North Carolina, and by the mid-1800s, they had formed the largest Scottish settlement in North America.

Beyond the names and the odd turn of phrase, little really remains in daily life of what must once have been a transplanted Celtic society in the Southeastern United States. These "Scots Irish," or Ulster Scots, mixed with Irish settlers and mingled with English, German, African, and Native American influences in the hollows of the Blue Ridge and the Smokies and across the foothills of the Alleghenies and the Cumberland Plateau. Time tempered the individual tang of their ways, and few of their enduring influences, you could argue, are discernible there today. If you have taken time to savor the music of the region, you may well argue to the contrary.

Scots Irish tunes like "Sally Gooden" and "Turkey in the Straw," and ballads like "The Devil and the Farmer's Wife" and "Down in the Willow Garden," are the footprints of the immigrants who settled across this countryside and combined Scottish, Irish, and English traditions in the Appalachian hollows.

Tunes, songs, and stories were handed down as faithfully as family names and changed a little, as did the names. Ever developing on the bows and strings of a musical people, the settlers' dance tunes spurred the old-time fiddle and banjo music of the South, bluegrass, and rockabilly. Their ballads formed the roots of early country music, and their stories the fertile soil of an eloquent tradition in the spoken and written word.

The culture of the Highland Scots in the lowlands of eastern North Carolina was undermined by the fervor of religious revivals, and then dispersed in an unpublicized twentieth-century clearance: the establishment of the enormous Army camp Fort Bragg. The small graveyard in the heart of the military complex is one of the few in the country containing gravestones with Gaelic inscriptions.

Had these forces not come to bear on the Gaelic-speaking community of eastern North Carolina, we might today have had a Cape Breton–style culture in that part of the South. As it is, the chief Celtic influence came from Lowland Scots in the Southern Highlands. In recent times, there has been a revival of interest in the connections between Appalachian and Celtic music, including the old-time fiddle music of the South. Tom Burton of East Tennessee State University surveyed the ten most common southern Appalachian ballads and noted that seven were of Scottish origin, including the three most popular.

Hammered dulcimer is one of the favored instruments among players of Celtic music in this region. Two handheld wooden hammers strike its metal strings, attached horizontally across a trapezoidal wooden box. Harp melodies are particularly suited to this instrument, which dates back to colonial times. The fretted or Appalachian dulcimer is a long, narrow instrument laid across the lap. Fingers of the left hand press on the strings, which are picked or strummed by the right hand. It has been used in the southern mountains since the eighteenth century. As singer, songwriter, and collector, Jean Ritchie has demonstrated, with its natural built-in drone, it is perfect for accompanying the old songs and ballads.

Exploring the musical heritage of the Appalachian Mountains and foothills offers an even broader appreciation of the roots and branches of Celtic musical traditions. Their hardy spirit has endured and adapted with great vigor across miles and generations, creating a fascinating new indigenous American music; a contemporary outgrowth from ancient roots.

Cecil Sharpe the Ballad Collector

Francis James Child is remembered in the United States as the most significant collector of ballads from the British Isles. But in 1916, a middle-aged Englishman named Cecil Sharpe (1859–1924) traveled to the United States and spent two years in rural Appalachia, collecting nearly two thousand songs and dances that underscored the strong links between traditional Appalachian and Celtic music. As they had been in the British Isles, songs and ballads were passed down in the mountain hollows by oral transmission. He collected in the tiny community of Sodom, hitting a particularly rich ballad vein in Marshall County, North Carolina.

Sharpe had begun pursuing his passion for preserving and documenting the traditions of British folk song in 1903. Traveling around rural England by bicycle, he began transcribing songs and dances from remote regions of the country. His archives, including the Appalachian collection, are accessible at Cecil Sharpe House in London.

FOUR

Celtic Music Deconstructed

I t's no surprise that the varieties of Celtic music share common elements. Bagpipes, in differing designs, are played in all the countries and regions. The harp and fiddle are the two other ubiquitous instrumental pillars of the music. Regardless of whether they are listening to a Welsh harp air or an Irish pipe jig, some listeners probably identify Celtic music by its instrumental characteristics alone: the drone of the pipes, the lilt of the fiddle, the bright trill of the tin whistle, the ringing strings of the harp. But considering the Greek bouzouki has become one of the instruments of choice for accompanying Celtic music since the 1970s, focusing on these sounds alone can be deceptive. To discover the heart of this music, we must listen beyond instrumental accents, exploring the music itself, along with playing styles and singing voices.

The Instruments

Variety in the music is generated as much by the pool of instruments traditionally used as it is by geography. From harp to bodhrán, the sound of string and skin both connects and differentiates the varieties of Celtic music.

Harp The harp was the ancient instrument of the aristocracy, from Ireland to Brittany, and professional harpers were held in high regard. Although the instrument struggled to retain its historical standing, it never lost its magical and mythical associations. So today the repertoire of the harp offers an important connection to the very beginnings of Celtic rooted music. It also creates some of the most contemporary of sounds, a place where Celtic music meets the world.

Small harps are common in South America, and the primitive harp, still found in Africa, was once widespread throughout the world. Nowadays, the grand-sounding pedal harp is standard in full orchestras. So what is distinctive about Celtic harps? First of all, we don't assume that the harp must only have found its way into the hands of the Atlantic Celts. It may be that the harp was independently born among the ancient people of the British Isles and Ireland and developed there.

By the eighth and ninth centuries, several different stringed instruments were being played in Scotland and Ireland. Images of triangular-framed harps were being carved onto Pictish stones on the east coast of Scotland in the eighth century. Irish carvings show lyres from this era, and the first triangular-framed harp shows up on a carved stone in Ireland in the twelfth century. So we know that harplike instruments have been played in Scotland and Ireland for more than twelve hundred years. The small harp, or *clarsach* (Scotland), *clairseach* (Ireland), *telyn* (Welsh), and *tellenn*

(Brittany), plays an important role in the culture of all the Celtic lands.

There are no pedals on small Celtic harps, and levers are sometimes now installed at the top of each string to allow sharps and flats to be played. In Wales, harp music followed its own path. Looking for a fully chromatic instrument, they imported the triple harp from Italy in the seventeenth century, with its three rows of strings. The two outside rows are equivalent to the white notes on a piano keyboard, and the inside row sustains the black chromatic notes. The Welsh alone proudly claim an unbroken tradition in harp dating back more than one thousand years.

Missionaries from Britain brought the harp to Armorica, now Brittany, and representations of the instrument there date from the eleventh century. Unfortunately, interest in the harp faded when Brittany lost its independence in the sixteenth century. As described earlier, the Breton harp was resurrected by Jord Cochevelou and taken to international audiences by his son Alan Stivell.

Most Celtic harps of today feature a single row of gut, nylon, or wire strings, which change the sound of the instrument. Nails are used for plucking the ringing metal strings, and fingertips for other types of harp. The earliest ancient specimen, the Brian Boru harp, dates from the thirteenth century and is housed in Trinity College, Dublin. Contemporary harp makers replicate ancient forms and use new technologies to develop the sound of the instrument. The electro-harp, pioneered by Stivell, is now a popular part of the remarkable worldwide revival enjoyed by these instruments today.

Traditionally, harpers would accompany epic poetry of great heroic and tragic tales. Their patrons expected them to be able to summon tears, laughter, and sleep. They played laments, lullabies, and formal, listening music that, in Scotland, may have provided the inspiration for the highly stylized theme and variation *ceol mor* bagpipe form. Theirs was the art music of their day, and, like many of the tradition bearers of the Celtic countries and regions, harpers considered it a point of pride that their music was not written down. They carried their tunes, poetry, and tales in memory, passing them orally from teacher to pupil, player to player. It may be that much of the older music composed for the harp was picked up on bagpipe and fiddle as the harp waned in popularity.

Today, harpers are as likely to share a dance tune repertoire with other instruments as they are to play more ancient melodies associated with their instrument. Popular in song accompaniment, today's sound reinforcement possibilities ensure that harps can compete and blend with much louder instruments—even bagpipes—when performed live or in the studio. Players such as Wendy Stewart, Savourna Stevenson, Sileas, Máire Brennan, Sedrenn, Máire Ni Chathasaigh, and Alan Stivell exploit this fully as they guide the Celtic harp toward jazz, world, and popular music without compromising its captivating Celtic identity.

The Belfast Harp Festival

The 1790s in Ireland saw the beginnings of modern Irish nationalism take root, accompanied by a cultural revival that injected momentum into efforts to document traditions in music and language. No one had ever transcribed the ancient music of the Irish harpers. This task fell to organist Edward Bunting, born in 1773 to an Irish mother and an English father. Belfast citizen Dr. James MacDonnell had organized a gathering of harpers in the city's Exchange Rooms, hoping to collect and preserve the national harp music of Ireland before it disappeared, and engaged Bunting to transcribe their music.

Ten harpers, six of whom were blind, attended the festival and played their tunes over a three-day period, from July 11 to 13, 1792. Ninety-seven-year-old Dennis Hempson (1695–1807) was the only harper present who played in the traditional Irish manner, plucking brass stings with long fingernails. It was the last time the great harpers of the age would play together, and Bunting was charged with the task of writing down their airs precisely, adding nothing to the melodies. The festival captured, just in time, the riches of an era of orally transmitted music reaching back centuries.

The melodies Bunting recorded at the Belfast Harp Festival were to form the core of his first volume of music, *General Collection of the Ancient Music of Ireland,* published in 1796. He traveled throughout the north of Ireland to complete his first volume and followed with two more in 1809 and 1840, including dances and pipe airs. The music they contained offered a glimpse of a passing age in rural Ireland, when music existed only as an oral tradition.

Bagpipes Bagpipes are heard throughout the world in massed military pipe bands and as solitary instruments of mourning. But the music of this powerful and varied set of instruments goes way beyond the stereotypes. Apart from the military marches of the Highland pipes, the rhythms of the dance floor—reels, jigs, and strathspeys—are now common to the pipers' repertoire. And perhaps no instrument in any musical genre delivers a lament or a slow air with quite the emotional authority of the pipes. This is one good reason why anyone who has yet to hear the bagpipes played by a top-class piper would be well advised to make the effort. The various bagpipe instruments should not be judged alone from the efforts of occasional, recreational pipers. Any instrument can make excruciating sounds when played poorly, and the pipes are no exception. When you hear the instrument played properly, you can only marvel at the quality of harmonic and tonal sounds achieved.

The bagpipes have a history spanning many hundreds of years and many parts of the world. Connecting hollow bones and sticks to an animal bag, bagpipes are thought to have been developed by shepherds such far-flung places as Hungary, Russia, the Czech Republic, Egypt, and India.

Throughout many designs, and whether mouth blown or bellows blown, the bag is inflated, squeezed, and supplies a continuous flow of air to the pipes, while the chanter is used to finger the tune. The various pipe styles vary in sound depending on the type of reeds used, the number of drones, and whether these are tuned at the same pitch or at varying intervals.

Some scholars believe bagpipes came to Britain with the Romans. They played them in religious ceremonies and for entertainment, though never in the military, as was eventually the case in Scotland. Emperor Nero (37–68 C.E.) famously played the bagpipes and the fiddle, although which instrument he chose to accompany the burning of Rome is anybody's guess. The Roman-style two-chanter instruments were never adopted by the indigenous people of the British Isles, however, and many historians speculate that bagpipes were in use long before the Roman invasion and occupation beginning 43 C.E. Either way, it is doubtful that they were maintained in continuous use from Roman times.

Pipers begin to appear on carved stones in Ireland between the ninth and eleventh centuries, and pictorial evidence shows them commonly used by minstrels in England in the tenth century. These primitive pipe instruments did not feature a bag, and early references to the more sophisticated instrument appear in Scotland in the twelfth century. Legend has it that the pipes were played by the Scots under King Robert the Bruce, when they defeated the English at the Battle of Bannockburn (1314).

Ceol Mor (Big Music)

The MacCrimmons were the hereditary pipers to the Clan MacLeod on the Isle of Skye. Apart from this known fact, much else written about the early days of the mysterious pipers comes from the realms of legend. Their origins are uncertain; however, it is known that they were educated, sophisticated, and successful farmers. They became great teachers and opened a college of piping on Skye in the seventeenth century. Clan chiefs would send their young pipers there, and they would embark on a twelve-year training program before graduating as fully fledged pipers, ready to assume their responsibilities. Their teachers taught the tunes orally by a vocal system known as *canntaireachd,* also believed to have been developed by the MacCrimmons.

Donald MacCrimmon (1570–1640) is the first to emerge in the history books. He was a piper and composer and is credited with inventing the classical music of the Scottish bagpipes, *piobaireachd,* or *ceol mor* (big music). The repertoire of dance tunes and songs, known as *ceol beag,* was popular in his day, as it is still. *Ceol beag* is developing all the time, from simple quicksteps to intricate competition marches and contemporary tunes often written in the old style. But *ceol mor* represented a significant departure in musical approach. It is a very complicated form of music, and it may have existed in some simpler structure before the MacCrimmons. In fact, there is some speculation that it may have been based upon the ancient repertoire of Scottish harp music.

Ceol mor is played along the lines of a theme and variations in three sections: the salute, the lament, and the gathering. The theme, or urlar, is played first, followed by the siubhal, the taorluath, the crunluath, then returns to the urlar again in closing. A piece of ceol mor develops over a lengthy performance, and each section is layered with increasing complexity. In bagpipe music, the form is unique and is considered to be one of the highest arts in all Celtic music.

The bagpipes in Scotland entered a difficult period after the failure of the 1745 Jacobite Rising under Bonnie Prince Charlie. Highland clans had always used it to accompany their advance and charge into battle. In the Disarming Act, passed by the British government of 1746, the carrying of arms and the wearing of the kilt were banned. The Highland pipes were seen as an instrument of war, and they were initially outlawed, too, then used as a means to raise Scottish regiments for foreign wars in the far reaches of the British Empire from the eighteenth to the twentieth century. It has taken the Highland pipes some time to enlarge upon their military image.

Other forms of Scottish bagpipe almost died out under the dominance of the Highland pipes. For its marching bands, the army preferred the louder, more portable mouth-blown variety to bellows-blown pipes. The decline in bellows-blown, or *cauld wind*, pipes was also aided by the shift in emphasis from the agricultural way of life (lowland pipes having been popular in rural areas such as the Borders of Scotland). The accordion took over from the pipes as the dancers' preferred accompaniment, with the fiddle.

Fortunately, players such as Robert Wallace, Gordon Mooney, and Hamish Moore, who also makes bellows-blown

Scottish bagpipes, have managed to save Scottish bellows piping from extinction and reestablished its place in Scottish music. In the early 1970s, Wallace and his fellow members of the group The Whistlebinkies started using these instruments, first recording them in 1976. The Lowland or Border pipes are similar in sound to the Highland pipes, but with less volume. Scottish small pipes are similar in sound to the bellows-blown Northumbrian pipes, currently enjoying a vigorous revival in their native lands of the northeast of England. Kathryn Tickell, Alasdair Anderson, and Ged Foley have all taken this engaging instrument to wide audiences.

The uilleann pipes are the distinctive Irish form of bagpipes and the most sophisticated of all these instruments. They were developed from the Irish equivalent of the Highland pipes around 1700. Someone seeing the uilleann pipes played for the first time can be amazed by the amount of activity involved—the piper is pumping bellows, keeping pressure on the bag under the arm; something is happening under the right wrist; and the fingers are working away at the melody.

The name uilleann came from the Irish word for elbow, because the bellows are attached to the player's elbow, then around the waist. This is how the air is provided, so no blowing is required, and an uilleann piper is always seated with the bag under his or her left arm. The instrument has a chanter with a musical range of two octaves and can produce semi-tones, too. The second octave is produced, as with a tin whistle or flute, by overblowing. Like Highland pipes, uilleann pipes have three drones; however, they are also uniquely designed with regulators. These are three pipes protruding from the main stock of the instrument, with a system of keys for providing accompaniment or harmony.

Developing the chanter reed, which produces the two

octaves (in contrast to the nine notes of the Highland pipes), was a big breakthrough in the eighteenth century. It was during this period that uilleann pipes evolved into what we see today, played by Paddy Moloney of The Chieftains, Liam O'Flynn, Paddy Keenan, Davy Spillane, and many more.

The vibration of wood; the droning effect; the raw, native sound, so close to how it was conceived in early times—all this combines to make the pipes produce a glorious musical effect. The music of the bagpipes, whether solo, in a Celtic band, or with an orchestra, has never enjoyed more exposure and popularity than it does today, and there is an enormous repertoire of tunes. Like the harp and fiddle, bagpipes create a musical link between all the Celtic lands, with Welsh pipes, the Breton biniou, and the Galician gaita, all continuing to sustain this ancient music into the twenty-first century.

Fiddle Along with the harp and pipes, the fiddle is one of the three instrumental pillars of traditional music from Celtic roots. It traveled to the New World with immigrants from throughout Europe, and from the seventeenth century, it took its place as the most popular dance instrument on both sides of the Atlantic. The American South in particular is known for its great fiddling traditions. Hanover County, Virginia, hosted the first fiddling contest in 1736, held on November 30 in honor of the holiday of St. Andrew, patron Saint of Scotland.

At one time, it was possible to tell an Irish fiddler's home county based solely on the accent of his fiddle. Regional styles have diluted somewhat since the advent of the recording era, as young fiddlers emulate the individual techniques of such influential players as Kevin Burke, Frankie Gavin, and Tommy Peoples. Repertoires do still highlight regional differences: Players from County Kerry will emphasize slides and polkas, whereas fiddlers from County Clare and County Galway, reared on the dancing traditions of these Western counties, will favor set dances, played in the distinctive, ornate styles of the region. Born in London of Sligo parentage, Kevin Burke insists there never was a Sligo musician who couldn't play "The Sligo Maid," "The Woman of the House," and "The Sailor's Bonnet." These tunes were certainly in the repertoire of the three fiddlers credited with establishing the "Sligo style" in the early twentieth century: Michael Coleman, James Morrison, and Paddy Killoran.

In general, we can say that Irish fiddling is highly decorated with grace notes and triplets, and players such as Martin Hayes from County Clare demonstrate the technique of ornamentation at its most developed.

Donegal in the north of Ireland has always had strong ties to Scotland, and the flavor of the Donegal fiddle is marked by a Scottish influence, with an echo of the bagpipe in the bowing style. Donegal highlands are based on Scottish strathspeys, stressing rhythm and placing less emphasis upon ornamentation. Mairead Ní Mhaonaigh of Altan bows with all the drive and passion of her native Donegal.

The most easily identifiable feature of Scottish fiddle styles is the use of the Scots snap: a pair of notes, the first short, the second longer, around which the strathspey dance rhythm is based. Scottish fiddlers play with a bouncier rhythm than their Irish counterparts, and reels and jigs are often played more evenly.

The fiddle has been played since the seventeenth century in Scotland. By the eighteenth century, the instrument was widely played by all classes and was also the central instrument of the ballrooms and drawing rooms of the gentry. This was the so-called Golden Age of Scottish fiddling, and more than fifteen hundred tunes were composed during this era, with Perthshire, in the heart of the country, considered the main hub of Scottish fiddle music (see the "Perthshire's Pride" sidebar on Niel Gow in Chapter 2, "The Story of Celtic Music"). Highland-style fiddling was also more widespread at this time, using open lower strings to mimic the drone of the bagpipe. Highland fiddling also imitates the inflections of the Gaelic language through the bowing ornamentation. Scottish fiddle music was established in Cape Breton, Nova Scotia, during its Golden Age. As a result, the old Highland style is preserved there today. In addition to the pipe drone and Gaelic lilt, it emphasizes a "driven bow," where equal effort is invested in the upward and downward strokes. Today, piano or guitar usually accompanies Cape Breton fiddlers such as Buddy and Natalie MacMaster and Jerry Holland, and their playing is closely allied to the rhythms and sequences of Cape Breton step dance.

In the Victorian age, the music became more gentrified in Scotland, and a classical influence took hold. With more than six hundred tunes to his name, James Scott Skinner, "The Strathspey King," was one of the most prolific composers of Scottish fiddle music. His northeast strathspey style combined a classical and traditional approach and influences many fiddlers today. The dancy, rhythmic approach to Scottish fiddling can be heard in the playing of Alasdair Fraser, Pete Clark, and the late Johnny Cunningham. Although they play mostly Scottish tunes, Jennifer Wrigley of Orkney and Catriona Macdonald and Aly Bain from Shetland communicate the Scandinavian influences of the Northern Isles fiddle styles.

In addition to the tunes of Skinner and Gow, Captain Simon Fraser's 1815 collection *Airs and Melodies Peculiar to the Highlands of Scotland,* is still a well-used resource for Scottish fiddlers. The Welsh fiddle repertoire has been preserved in manuscripts from the eighteenth and nine-teenth centuries, containing many tunes that appear very similar in style to contemporary classical or popular music. Although there is an unbroken tradition of Welsh harp play-ing, it isn't clear how the fiddle was played in Wales in the nineteenth or even the early twentieth centuries. So it is nec-essary to look back at how the music was actually recorded in the manuscripts, hoping that it may be possible to clarify how Welsh fiddlers used to play.

Through their work in the Welsh bands Ar Log and 4 Yn Y Bar, Steven Rees and Huw Roberts were determined to place Welsh fiddle music alongside the vibrant fiddle tradi-tions of Ireland and Scotland. They have researched many Welsh collections, with the Morris Edwards manuscript in particular unveiling listening tunes and dance tunes, espe-cially minuets and jigs. In contrast to Ireland and Scotland, Welsh music doesn't include the reel as a dance form, al-though there are plenty of marches and hornpipes. Welsh collectors seem to have followed no national agenda, writing down tunes they simply liked to play, including some also contained in Playford's English publications and Scottish tunes such as "The Flowers of Edinburgh."

In May 1997, the First Welsh Fiddle Convention brought together like-minded Welsh musicians and fiddlers. Further gatherings have added momentum to the resurgence of tradi-tional music in Wales in general, while raising the profile of the fiddle in Wales.

Whistle and Flute Archaeologists working in Germany recently discovered a bone flute made more than forty thousand years ago. The find would have been of interest to any flute player, and also to inhabitants of the northern Orkney Isles. Their Neolithic forebears left behind a bone flute fragment in

2300 B.C.E., and this is the oldest musical artifact found to date in Scotland.

Inexpensive and portable, the tin whistle is perhaps the most modest instrument in Celtic music, although it has a venerable history, dating back a thousand years or more. Dubliner Mary Bergin plays this instrument with remarkable breath control and dexterity, and other expressive practitioners include Paddy Moloney of The Chieftains, and Bronx-born Joanie Madden of Cherish the Ladies.

The modern transverse flute was developed in more recent centuries and imported to the British Isles from the European mainland. The painted ceiling at Crathes Castle in Aberdeenshire in the northeast of Scotland dates from 1599. It shows a minstrel playing a transverse flute, and there were probably earlier instruments of that sort played in the country. It was certainly popular by the eighteenth century, when Oswald's *Pocket Companion* and other collections of Scottish music included flute versions of fiddle tunes. Daniel Dow's 1776 music collection also offers flute arrangements, including one of a *piobaireachd* composed for Highland pipes and rarely heard played on other instruments.

The flute is well suited to the techniques of ornamenting melodies and as such has been very popular in Ireland since the eighteenth century. Unlike the orchestral concert flute, this is a wooden instrument with a gentler, breathier tone. Anyone who wants to hear its expressive qualities at their finest should listen to Irish players Cathal McConnell of Boys of the Lough, or Matt Molloy of The Chieftains. Jean-Michel Veillon has used his instrument to great effect in unlocking the unique rhythms and hypnotic melodies of Breton music. Nova Scotia native Chris Norman has dedicated himself to reviving traditional flute music and playing styles from Scotland and Canada.

Accordion, Button Box, and Concertina Few instruments have as unassuming origins as the accordion. In 1829, an Austrian piano tuner was looking for a device to assist him at his work. Two boxes, bellows, and a set of piano keys later, the accordion was born. The modern instrument has buttons or keys pressed by the right hand, allowing air to travel across flat metal reeds. One reed sounds when pushing the bellows, another when they are pulled, while the left hand plays accompaniment with bass notes and chords.

The piano accordion, favored in Scottish country dance and folk bands, has a full chromatic piano keyboard. Irish players prefer the lively button box or button accordion, in designs ranging from one row diatonic to five rows in a chromatic scale.

The concertina is a small free-reed instrument related to the accordion. It was developed in England in 1830 by Charles Wheatstone and quickly found a role in music halls, on sailing ships, with dance groups, and with traveling buskers. Like the accordion, the portable concertina is played by expanding and compressing bellows. English concertinas are fully chromatic, while Anglo concertinas depend on the push and pull of the bellows to play different notes, which gives them a bouncier sound, preferred by some musicians.

Phil Cunningham, Joe Burke, Jackie Daly, Karen Tweed, John Whelan, Sharon Shannon, Alan Pennec, and Simon Thoumire have all expanded the eloquence of accordions and concertinas since they were first adapted to traditional dance music in the early twentieth century. Throughout Ireland, Scotland, England, and Brittany, contemporary Celtic players add a lush, atmospheric accompaniment to singing, bring an easy lull to slow airs and waltzes, and deliver a light and lively lead in the melodies of jigs, reels, and hornpipes.

Bouzouki Playing at the time with the group Sweeney's Men, Irish string player Johnny Moynihan brought a bouzouki back from Greece in the early 1970s and gave it as a gift to Alec Finn of the group De Danann. Finn was a key influence in developing this long-necked Greek folk instrument for Irish music, along with other early innovative players, Dónal Lunny and Andy Irvine, who still use it as their main instrument.

The bouzouki is now standard in many groups. Celtic musicians from Brittany to Ireland, Scotland, and beyond have created a boon for string instrument builders throughout the British Isles, Ireland, and the United States, who have responded with finely crafted bouzoukis, sometimes known as the octave mandolin, as it is generally tuned an octave below the mandolin (GDAE). Injecting rhythm, picking counter-melodies, offering chords, and strumming a drone, Celtic musicians favor open tunings for the bouzouki to complement the modal sound of much of their music. Along with the banjo, the mandolin, and the guitar, they have employed their natural aptitude to adapt this recent import to their needs and develop their music. The bouzouki is now at the core of the Celtic sound.

Bodhrán This traditional Irish frame drum has become the ubiquitous percussion instrument of Celtic music. Seán Ó Riada was the first to explore its potential in traditional ensembles in the 1960s, although it was heard on some Irish music recordings as early as the 1920s.

The Chieftains spread the beat of the bodhrán internationally, abandoning the more common ceilidh-style stick drum, and it has been a standard rhythmic pulse through Celtic music ever since. The Corries introduced it to Scottish music in the 1960s, and Johnny McDonagh, Dónal Lunny, and Jim

Sutherland have developed its unexpected potential through sensitive and individual approaches. Tommy Hayes is widely regarded as a creative genius on this apparently simple instrument.

Traditionally made with goatskin and a wooden rim and struck with a simple stick beater, the bodhrán adds great drive to a recording or performance. Etiquette dictates that players should be sensitive when introducing the bodhrán to a session. The unspoken rule is: one at a time, please.

Dance Music

When we hear traditional instrumental music from Celtic roots these days, it is often presented as a staged performance. Yet so much of this music is Scottish, Irish, Welsh, Breton, or Galician dance music, and only recently has it been so likely to be showcased separately from the dances themselves. The melodies are certainly engaging enough to stand alone. And the bands bringing them to us arrange the tunes in imaginative, often high-speed sets that would defeat the stamina of even the most adventurous and athletic of dancers. So although ceilidh dancing and ceilidh bands have thrived at dance halls and festivals, the theatrical performance of "Celtic music," in its broadest sense, has been evolving apart from the dances with which it was once so closely bound.

In recent years, Irish bands have led the way in reuniting the music with the dance in performance settings. The Chieftains were first to do this onstage with Irish step dance, touring with a young Michael Flately in the early 1980s.

Cherish the Ladies always perform with Irish step dance pairs or teams, and have done so since before the popularity of the form soared with Bill Whelan's *Riverdance* phenomenon in the 1990s. Now Scottish musicians and dancers are realizing the importance of building upon the tremendous popularity of ceilidh and country dancing and the reawakened interest in Scottish step dance, by placing their dance traditions center stage. And so the trend spreads. Reunited in this way, the bond between traditions in dance and music is manifest, and their linked performance offers us a new dimension in Celtic music.

The social dance music of the Celtic countries and regions varies in style and tempo from country to country, but the tunes have one thing in common: They are accessible, repetitive, and cyclical, and they exert an incontestable invitation to take to the floor. Formal forms of dance, especially Irish step dance, now draw huge audiences who sit, watch, and marvel at the footwork. But most of the dance activities throughout Celtic countries and regions are social occasions. Those who lack knowledge of the figures followed in each dance are cheerfully guided on the arms of partners and by callers' instructions.

Jigs and reels are particularly common in both Scottish and Irish country and set dance music. The jig was popularized in the sixteenth century and is the oldest of the Irish dance tunes, although eighteenth- and nineteenth-century fiddlers and pipers composed most of the jigs we know today. Jigs are sprightly and cheery in character and are played in four time signatures: a single jig in 6/8, a double also in 6/8 but with an eighth note voiced, a slip jig in 9/8, and a straight jig in 2/4 time. (In Galicia, the muiñeira is a 6/4 jig rhythm.)

The reel, originating in Scotland in the middle of the seventeenth century, is the most popular social dance rhythm. Danced in 4/4 time, the music consists of four or eight measures, repeated over and over.

Slower than a reel, the hornpipe reputedly originated in England in the sixteenth century and is now a fixture in Irish dance. The word *hornpipe* derives from an early double reed wind instrument made from animal horn. Early versions of this dance are in 3/2 time, but today the hornpipe is usually played in 2/4 and 4/4 meter.

Scotland's dances feature the indigenous rhythm of the strathspey. This is like a slow reel in 4/4 time but is played with a distinctive restrained skip, or Scots snap, that is reflected in the steps on the dance floor. The simple, strong rhythms of marches in 2/4 time, usually danced in couples, are also popular in Scotland.

Strathspeys have found popularity in the north of Ireland, especially Donegal, where musical traditions have been traded with Scotland for centuries. Donegal tunes called "highlands" are derived from Scottish strathspeys and are played in 4/4 time. Slip jigs, in 9/8 time, are also abundant in Donegal, and the county has a tradition of mazurkas, dances of Polish lineage, possibly imported by soldiers returning from foreign campaigns. Some waltzes in Celtic music are likely to have been absorbed by the same process, although Scotland and Cape Breton have robust indigenous traditions of this dance type.

In the Irish counties of Kerry and Cork, polkas and slides are popular. Polkas are fast dances in 2/4 time, and slides are very similar to single jigs only played a little faster and with a more exaggerated rhythm.

Brittany has its own dance rhythms and patterns, twenty-five in all, and these are featured in the hypnotic circle and chain dances that pulse into the night at a Breton ceilidh, a *fest-noz*.

The sense of fun that pervades any gathering like this is addictive. Whether dancing in couples, or in sets of six, eight, or more, Celtic ceilidh, country, and set dancing allows you to look at, speak to, touch, and laugh with your partners. The lights are on. You can see. And it's interesting to note that the number of young people attending ceilidh dances has grown enormously in recent years.

The music itself clearly contributes common elements to the Celtic sound, but it becomes difficult to separate structure from emotional response. Most listeners say they respond to the "ancient," "haunting," "minor" quality in some of the melodies. Are they moved by the scales around which much of the music sits—the church modes often used in Gregorian chants and other medieval and renaissance music? Celtic music is structured around only four of these modes, but not uniquely so, as they are also used in other traditions of the world's ethnic music. Some Celtic tunes are played on fewer than seven notes, including some in pentatonic (five-note) modes. Chinese music is also based around a pentatonic mode, and we might easily encounter this quality in music from Eastern Europe, the Middle East, and Africa. So is it the drone underpinning much of the music that creates that unique Celtic sound: the harmonic and tonal quality of the pipes, the vibration? Maybe, but again, this is hardly exclusive. Indian music shares a droning quality through the sitar, and what could issue a more earthy, resonating drone than the Australian digeridoo?

Nonmusical elements are clearly as important to the sound, and the spirit, of Celtic music. Whether it's a cheerful fiddle melody or a pipe lament, the music seems always to provide a powerful emotional outlet. It can grip you in a fit of melancholy and lift you, just as easily, in a burst of joy. As the music comes from the heart, so does your response. And if this is true of the instrumental music, it is doubly so of the quality of the Celtic voice. Indeed, much of the instrumental styles and especially the grace notes used in pipe and fiddle music have evolved around the nuances and inflections of the ancient Celtic languages.

Celtic Voices

The appeal of this music is no more apparent than it is the moment a Celtic language or dialect is expressed in song. Language is no barrier. Songs fill the listener with pride, emotion, compassion, and joy and come from traditions that have often been sustained orally for centuries. Fourteenth-century Scottish bard John Barbour wrote that he saw no need to record for posterity the details of a particular battle because the women were already singing about it. He was so convinced the incident would be remembered through their song alone that he didn't even bother to identify the battle or record any of its details. His faith in the potency of the tradition was well placed. Countless ballads and folk songs were passed down through the ages with their dramatic pattern and climax intact, even as details were localized or discarded.

It's important to say that singing was not traditionally about performance for its own sake. The songs themselves were considered more important than individual singers. The Battle of Harlaw was fought in Scotland in 1411, and the ballad by the same name tells the story of the confrontation between the Scots and the English. It is still sung today because for six centuries, many people who would not have considered themselves "singers" handed it down, in families, among communities. Ballads and songs, *gwerz* in Brittany, traveled through the centuries on that reliable vehicle called oral transmission. This is not to say that they didn't change. Another characteristic common to all Celtic music, across instrumental and vocal traditions, is the tolerance of variation and improvisation. Anyone, at any time, has always been allowed to have his or her own version of a song or melody. There is no right way. A tune or song may become one's own by application of technique, grace notes, and even local dialect.

This is one of the reasons the tradition is so rich and so alive. Indeed, different versions of the same music might spring up in Ireland and Scotland, or in Brittany and Wales.

Ornamentation is another musical device common to all Celtic singing and instrumental styles. A melody may be quite simple, but notes may be varied, extended, stopped, cut, and blurred in a style unique to the individual or their home region. This is most common in Irish *sean nós* (old style) singing, thought to be the most ancient form of Irish music. Like almost all traditional Celtic song styles, it is a cappella and allows the narrative of the song to lead the singer among the decoration of grace notes and other vocal ornamentations. In its intricate vocal patterns, it is almost reminiscent of the complex footwork used in Irish dance.

Highly valued in Scottish and Irish traditional singing circles, itinerant families, the Travelers, kept alive a treasure trove of ancient songs and stories in one of the oldest oral cultures in Europe. When Travelers sing, some are credited with delivering a song in a manner that vents emotion in the listener and makes the hairs stand up on the back of the neck. Scottish Travelers call this quality the *conyach*, and it is common across Celtic traditional singing styles. It is about honesty, passion, connection to the past, and an ability to let the song speak through the singer. Jean Redpath made this point about Scots song, but it easily applies to all the Celtic vocal traditions: "We are a very emotional race—a bunch of incurable romantics—but whether by training or whether by some quirk of national personality, there's something that you find in common with most of the Celtic and most of the Northern European countries: a moody edge to the country. There's a feeling that the hardships folk have gone through just to scrape a living off the surface of the land have produced a certain kind of personality: a creature pretty well seasoned, wildly emotional, but so disciplined that it's not possible to let that emotion out through any other channel but through the music."

The Musical Community

It is misleading to separate the traditions in music, dance, and song even for the purposes of this discussion. These traditions intermingle. The song influences the instrumental music, instrumental work inspires song styles, dance is fed by the music, which in turn drives the dance. In Wales, an ancient form of music called *pennillion* fuses the sound of singer and harper, though each simultaneously performs a different melody. In Brittany, *kan ha diskan* is a call-and-response style of singing that can fuel a round of dancing for as long as the singers hold out. In Ireland, *diddling* or *lilting* is used to vocalize tunes. The most highly developed such art is to be found in Scotland, where Gaelic mouth music, or *puirt a beul,* creates complex vocables in the Gaelic tongue that mimic pipe music and provide rhythms for dancing. It was a great way to keep the ceilidh going during long periods when musical instruments were kept quiet for reasons of political reprisal or religious fervor.

Earlier we mentioned how many Irish melodies were rescued through the efforts of collector Francis O'Neill, and how much traditional Scots song owes to the genius of Robert Burns. As important as the repertoire clearly is, the spirit of wanting to participate in music making, or of wanting to share songs, is of equal interest to those who make Celtic music. Even the most dedicated traditional players and singers will not restrict themselves to a traditional repertoire. And this gets to the heart of the role of music in these communities. It has always been about bringing people together. It has often accompanied the toil and tedium of daily life, exploring its ordinary details. It has preserved personal stories of trial and tragedy and celebrated tales of heroism. It has reflected a heartfelt connection to place and a love of the land. The tradition remains strong because just as the past is remembered and older musical styles revered, so the new is embraced as a relevant part of contemporary life and work. Whether heard in a pub session, seen in the concert hall, or experienced on the dance floor, this is the substance of the living tradition of Celtic music.

FIVE

The Musicians

A throng of individuals, many unsung, breathe life into the diverse music we celebrate in this book. Selecting a limited number for mention in this chapter is difficult, but here are some of the personalities who have shaped, and still set the course for, the evolving traditions of Celtic music.

Altan (founded 1987): To discover the music of Altan is to discover the heart and soul of Irish music. The band has consciously worked to deliver an uncompromised blend of musical traditions, playing all the while with great passion and drive. Care is taken with the imaginative arrangement of each tune set or song, yet the result manages to convey the energy and joy of an unstructured Irish music session at its very best. The band has dominated the traditional Irish music scene since they first formed, and they are considered by many, including *The Irish Voice,* to be "quite simply the best Irish traditional band active on either side of the Atlantic."

The name of the band comes from Loch Altan, a lake near Gaoth Dobhair (Gweedore) in Irish-speaking Northwest Donegal. This is the birthplace of singer and fiddler Mairéad Ní Mhaonaigh. Her father, fiddler Proinsias O'Maonaig, is a leading figure in preserving and promoting Donegal fiddle music, which Ní Mhaonaigh and Altan have helped to popularize internationally.

Altan grew from the husband and wife duo of Mairéad Ní Mhaonaigh and the late Frankie Kennedy. With his masterful flute playing and his dedication to arranging Irish music with great deference for tradition, Kennedy's contribution to the sound of Altan was vital from the earliest days of the band. His infectious spirit and great humor are still palpable in the music of Altan.

The quick, single-stroke bowing and staccato triplets favored by Donegal fiddlers lies at the heart of the twin fiddling of Ní Mhaonaigh and Ciaran Tourish. The subtle, surefire button accordion playing of Dermot Byrne enhances this core of Altan's instrumental sound. Highly dynamic rhythm accompaniment comes from the bouzouki of Ciaran Curran and the guitars of Mark Kelly and Daithi Sproule. Mark and Daithi are alternate band members. When Altan tours in the United States, it's Connecticut-based Daithi who plays guitar and sings. Along with the passionate instrumentals, the impressive voice of Mairéad Ní Mhaonaigh gives the band its singular character. She offers songs in Irish and English with a voice of rare clarity and real feeling that grows in depth with each recording. *The Best of Altan* includes a bonus live CD from a 1989 concert in Germany and draws upon the band's first five albums.

Dan Ar Braz (b. 1949): This master Breton guitarist first explored folk-rock as part of Alan Stivell's band in the 1970s. He also worked with other legendary French and English folk-rock outfits Malicorne and Fairport Convention. Since those days, he has concentrated on developing his unique guitar style and composing music connecting Brittany's Celtic roots with Scotland, Ireland, and Galicia. Ar Braz creates epic Pan-Celtic works involving Scottish and Breton pipe bands with some of the most respected artists in Celtic music, including Dónal Lunny, Karen Matheson, Nollaig Casey, Jean Michel Veillon, and Donald Shaw. *Made in Breizh* samples from previous albums by Ar Braz, including *Theme for the Green Lands* and *Héritage Des Celtes*. While the music of Breizh, Brittany, is at the heart of Ar Braz's work, in inspiration and instrumentation he is celebrating inter-Celtic exchange to mighty effect.

Aly Bain (b. 1946): Shetland's best-known fiddler played with Boys of the Lough for nearly three decades from 1971. He was a pupil of the legendary teacher Tom Anderson, who restored popularity and pride to the musical traditions of Shetland fiddling. Since those days, virtuoso fiddler Bain has carried this message throughout the world with Boys of the Lough (with accordion player Phil Cunningham) and in television programs through which he has explored ethnic fiddle traditions from Shetland to North America. *Follow the Moonstone*, Bain's collaboration with composer and arranger Henning Sommero and the BT Scottish ensemble, is a spellbinding foray into the musical traditions of Scotland and Norway, connected through Bain's beloved Shetland.

Battlefield Band (formed 1969): Battlefield Band exerts an influential and lasting impact on contemporary Scottish traditional music, having been voted Best Live Act in the 2003 Scottish Traditional Music Awards. Along with Silly Wizard and the Tannahill Weavers, Battlefield Band helped rediscover and invigorate the music, being among the first to experiment with electric keyboards and apply rock 'n' roll energy to their bagpipe and fiddle arrangements. In more than three decades of touring, the band has built a deeply loyal worldwide following.

Battlefield Band has seen numerous personnel changes over the years, using the movement of players and singers through the lineup to rejuvenate the band's sound and repertoire. Through the decades, these have included such great names as co-founder Brian McNeill, Jamie McMenemy, Duncan MacGillivray, Ged Foley, Dougie Pincock, John McCusker, Iain MacDonald, Karine Polwart, and the late Davy Steele, among others. Singer, songwriter, and keyboard player Alan Reid has provided continuity in Battlefield Band since the very beginning and continues to lead their world travels today, with Mike Katz on pipes, Alasdair White on fiddle, and returning Battlefield alumnus Pat Kilbride on vocals, cittern, and other strings.

Although they already had three British releases under their belts, *Home Is Where the Van Is* recalls a special lineup of the band. In addition to co-founders Alan Reid and Brian McNeill, it features the guitar and sweet-sounding Northumbrian pipes of Ged Foley, now with The House Band and Patrick Street. Duncan MacGillivray was the piper for this recording, and his playing on Highland pipes, whistle, and harmonica is some of the most musical you'll hear.

Martyn Bennett (b. 1971): Born in Newfoundland and raised in the Scottish Highlands, Bennett blends his own remarkable piping, fiddling, and multi-instrumental artistry with the rhythms of hip-hop, dance, and house music and is one of Scotland's most inventive musicians in any genre. He attended a school for musically gifted children and was trained in classical violin and piano at the Royal Scottish Academy of Music and Drama. Bennett has since written music for string quartets, composed for the theater, and performed before eighty thousand people at Edinburgh's Hogmanay celebrations. *Bothy Culture* is a trailblazing hybrid album of Gaelic traditional, house, and hip-hop samples and rhythms and takes the idea of Celtic world music further than you may expect, with great humor and spirit.

Bennett's music defies categorization. Those who try have coined such terms as "croft kitchen ceilidh grooves on Afro-Islamic dread dirge dub jungle jazz trip hop"! Although battling serious illness, Bennett has recently continued to develop his interests in setting traditional voices, including those of his mother, Gaelic singer Margaret Bennett, and legendary Scots ballad singer and Traveler Sheila Stewart, against the textures of techno backing tracks.

Mary Bergin (b. 1949): This Dublin-born musician is revered for her remarkable technique on Irish tin whistle, having won the All-Ireland whistle title in her late teens. She has since taken her instrument to new heights and set the standard for whistle playing over the last three decades. Bergin has toured with De Dannan and the uilleann pipes and harp duo Joe and Antoinette McKenna. In 1991, she formed the trio Dordan with harper Kathleen Loughnane and fiddler Dearbhill Standun, playing a perfectly balanced blend of baroque and traditional Irish music.

Bergin's debut album, *Feadoga Stain*, marked a sea change for the whistle and raised its status in Irish traditional music. Backed by Johnny McDonough on bodhrán and Alec Finn's bouzouki, this collection of tunes showcases Bergin's stunning technique. *The Night Before...A Celtic Christmas,* Dordan's holiday album, blends traditional and original Irish music for the season to create an original, fresh Christmas collection.

Mary Black (b. 1955): One of the best-known Irish singing voices, Mary Black got her start with her brothers and sisters in the pubs of Dublin. The 1970s saw her fronting the band General Humbert, and she continued, mostly in the traditional vein, with De Dannan in the 1980s. Since then she has built a solo career around the work of contemporary songwriters from Ireland and beyond and has won great praise for her best-selling recordings, being voted Ireland's "best female artist" of 1987 and 1988.

In *Collected,* Black's personal, contemporary approach to traditional material is on display along with her talent for selecting material ideally suited to her. *No Frontiers* includes enticing interpretations of new songs, mostly from Irish writers, and remained in the top thirty of the Irish album chart for more than a year.

Blazin' Fiddles (formed 1998): This potent group of fiddlers first came together for one short tour designed to showcase six of the regional fiddle styles of the Scottish Highlands and Islands. The tour was a huge success, and the band stayed together. Catriona Macdonald, protégé of revered fiddle teacher Tom Anderson, contributes the Shetland dialect to the ensemble, which also includes Bruce MacGregor, Aiden O'Rourke, Alan Henderson, and Iain MacFarlane, representing a remarkable diversity of styles. The resulting sound, backed by guitar and piano, is dynamic and youthful, and the sense of fun overflows from the recordings and concert performances. Fiery old tunes and elegant new compositions dwell side by side on *The Old Style*. The album benefits from the involvement of award-winning producer John McCusker, a fiddler himself, who brought the band to his home studio to record and managed to capture the mood of a Blazin' Fiddles live set.

Luka Bloom (b. 1955): Starting his musical life in the pubs of Dublin, Barry Moore moved to the Washington, D.C., area in 1987, when he changed his name to Luka Bloom and became a favorite on the U.S. East Coast acoustic music scene. Now re-settled in Ireland, his style is probably best described as Irish folk rock, and he is noted for his exhilarating guitar playing, introspective songs, and charismatic singing. He is the younger brother of singer-songwriter Christy Moore. Christy and the Hothouse Flowers join Bloom on *The Acoustic Motorbike*, an album of mostly original material presented with a particular Irish soulfulness, power, and passion.

The Bothy Band (formed 1975; disbanded 1979): February 2, 1975, was a milestone in Irish music. Six musicians, Dónal Lunny (bouzouki), Paddy Keenan (uilleann pipes), Matt Molloy (flute), Mícheál Ó Domhnaill (vocals and guitar), Tríona Ní Dhomhnaill (vocals and clavinet), and Tommy Peoples (fiddle), made their debut together at Trinity College, Dublin, and the legend of The Bothy Band was born. By the time of the County Sligo's Ballysadare Festival in 1979, the band was making its farewell appearance, with fiddler Kevin Burke having replaced Peoples in 1976. The first Irish group to bring the power of rock music to traditional dance tunes and instruments, the impact of The Bothy Band has reverberated internationally ever since.

Dónal Lunny had formed the band after leaving Planxty, and through this lineup, is credited with having brought a new, contemporary vigour to traditional music. The instrumental combination was largely traditional and acoustic through the tune sets and songs on the band's four original albums. *After-hours* is a live concert recording made in 1978 at the Palais des Arts in Paris and fully captures the onstage excitement and audience devotion enjoyed by The Bothy Band. All their recordings have created a must-learn repertoire for aspiring musicians in Ireland and beyond and are considered classics today. Meanwhile, each former member of The Bothy Band continues to play a key role in the evolving traditions of Celtic music.

Robin Huw Bowen (b. 1957): The only full-time professional triple harper has taken this unique Welsh instrument to audiences across the globe, both as a solo artist and with the traditional quartet Crasdant. He possesses a vast knowledge of the history and repertoire of the triple harp, the national instrument of Wales, and has collected many traditional Welsh tunes, some of which appear in his book of hornpipes. With three rows of parallel strings, the triple harp requires a particular dexterity of the player. Bowen's technique is exceptional, as is his ability to apply the theme and variation approach popular in traditional Welsh harp music. In *Harp Music of Wales,* Bowen recorded a wide selection of well-known traditional tunes, along with some new material written for harp. Bowen combines forces with Ann Morgan Jones and Sue Jones Davies in *Cusan Tan—Kiss of Fire* to present sensuous new songs and instrumentals for cello, flute, harp and voice.

Boys of the Lough (formed 1967): With performances and recordings reaching into five decades, this band is one of the most highly respected throughout all traditional music. Offering a blend of Irish and Scottish tunes and songs, Boys of the

Lough pioneered Celtic music with an international audience. The band's travels have been extensive since their first tour in 1967.

Fiddle, flute, piping, and vocal traditions combine through longtime members Dave Richardson (concertina, mandolin, accordion, and cittern) and Cathal McConnell (flute, whistle, and vocals). Newer recruit, guitarist Malcolm Stitt, provides the rhythmic drive in dance tunes and sensitive accompaniment in slow airs and songs. The rich flavors of Shetland fiddle music have been a constant feature for the band, a legacy of Aly Bain, who was a member of Boys of the Lough for thirty years and continues his varied career through other projects. Shetlander Kevin Henderson sustains this tradition in the current lineup.

Their *Farewell and Remember Me* was recorded during uilleann piper and singer Christy O'Leary's time with the band, and the album has both O'Leary and McConnell in particularly fine voice, flanked by a great selection of Irish and Scottish dance tunes. *Lonesome Blues and Dancing Shoes* features longtime members of the band, Richardson and McConnell, joined by Ireland's Brendan Begley on accordion and vocals and Scottish guitar and bouzouki powerhouse Malcolm Stitt for a classic collection of dance tunes and songs of parting.

Paul Brady (b. 1947): From County Tyrone in Northern Ireland, Brady's musical journey began in 1964, when he was studying at University College, Dublin. The city's rhythm and blues boom proved irresistible to him, and he was soon playing guitar and singing in local bands. Gradually the old songs and ballads of his own country, which were also being nurtured in student bars and coffeehouses, began to captivate him. His growing involvement with more traditional material led to an invitation to join The Johnstons, an extremely popular Irish folk group, known for their pure harmonies and eclectic repertoire, and also featuring singer, tenor banjo, and mandolin great Mick Moloney. Along with traditional music, they covered songs by Ewan McColl, Joni Mitchell, and Gordon Lightfoot. Soon Paul Brady was writing his own songs, too.

In 1974, Paul joined Planxty. This involvement, and a landmark duet recording with Andy Irvine on *Andy Irvine and Paul Brady* (see Chapter 7, "Celtic Music on CD"), kept his songwriting and contemporary music on the back burner for the remainder of the decade. However, by 1981 he released his first album of original songs. Since then, Paul Brady has toured with Dire Straits and Eric Clapton, topping the critics' poll in Ireland's Hot Press Awards in 1986. It did not take long for word of his songwriting skills to travel. Now his work has been covered by an impressive array of performers: Santana, Tina Turner, David Crosby, Dan Seals, Maura O'Connell, and Dolores Keane.

His own recording, *Trick or Treat,* features a duet with Bonnie Raitt, who had a hit of her own with a Brady song, "Not the Only One." More recently, Paul Brady has been embracing his earlier material, too. *Nobody Knows—The Best of Paul Brady* samples from Brady's many recordings and includes some of his best work. Included is a reprise of his classic "Arthur McBride," re-recorded twenty-five years after Brady first released the song on his revered album with Andy Irvine.

Whether in the field of traditional or contemporary song, Brady's impact on Irish and Celtic music has been enormous.

Máire Brennan (*see* Clannad).

Antonio Breschi (Antóni O'Breskey) (b. 1950): As an outsider to Celtic music, Antonio Breschi has illuminated new pathways in the unfolding story of this music, imagining its meeting place with World Music as early as the mid-1970s.

The categories of "World" and "New Age" music did not exist when Breschi began his trailblazing journey, yet he was first to combine Flamenco, Basque, Arabic, Latin, and Irish elements, his virtuoso jazz-styled piano uniting these traditions in remarkably original compositions. In 1984, he presented his fusion of Irish, Flamenco, and jazz styles on Italian television. His inclusion of a Flamenco dancer in the performance was a flash of brilliance and the first time anyone had explored the compatibility of Irish and Flamenco traditions.

A native of Florence, Breschi has been playing jazz and classical piano since he was three years old. He is acclaimed in his Italian homeland and also in Spain, where he traces a Flamenco heritage through his mother. His biggest musical impact, however, has undoubtedly been in Ireland, where he has collaborated with the legendary singer Ronnie Drew, accordionist Máirtin O'Connor, and many more artists in numerous visits to his adopted home. Pianist Mícheál O'Súilleabháin has advanced Breschi's use of piano in Irish traditional music, and Bill Whelan developed Breschi's synthesis of Flamenco, jazz, and Irish traditional strands as a key structure in his Irish music and dance spectacular, *Riverdance.*

The Colours of Music: 25 Years of the Music of Antóni O'Breskey is an overview of a unique anthology titled "The Ethnic Piano Collection." It offers music recorded in Ireland, Italy, Spain, and the Basque Country between 1975 and 1999, with guest performances by an international retinue, and is the perfect introduction to this innovative artist. A love of Irish music and friendships sparked his whimsical name change from Antonio Breschi to Antóni O'Breskey in the late 1990s.

Robin Bullock (b. 1964): Bullock's music accents the connections between Celtic and American traditional and acoustic music. That he is able to do so by playing almost any stringed instrument to perfection is his specialty. Thanks to multi-tracking, guitar, mandolin, cittern, bass guitar, fiddle, whistle, and piano are all in his recording repertoire. Bullock's second solo album, *Midnight Howl*, fully actualizes its subtitle: "A celebration of the wild American spirit and its roots in traditional, Irish, and Old-Time music." Bullock was a popular fixture in the Washington, D.C.–area acoustic scene, playing with the trio Helicon and Walt Michael, but he has been living in Paris in recent years, returning often to the United States to perform and teach.

Kevin Burke (b. 1950): Born in London, Kevin Burke's parents were from County Sligo. The distinctive fiddle styles of Sligo and neighboring Clare were commonly heard among the London Irish musical community, and these were the main influences feeding Burke's own developing style in the 1950s and '60s. He joined The Bothy Band in 1976, and after the group disbanded, he formed a very successful duo with guitarist Mícheál Ó Domhnaill through the early 1980s. Together they recorded *Portland*, which features some great medleys of reels and jigs.

By 1987, Burke had become involved with another band, Patrick Street. Based in Portland, Oregon, for more than two decades, Kevin Burke is one of the busiest Irish musicians around and can also be heard performing with Open House and the Celtic Fiddle Festival. *If the Cap Fits* features tunes from Sligo, Clare, and Kerry and culminates in a sixteen-minute-long reel medley, featuring Burke and various accompanists. His fluid, effortless fiddling has exerted a great influence on a generation of players in Ireland and beyond.

Capercaillie (formed 1983): The seeds of this band were sown at high school in Oban in the West Highlands of Scotland. The young lineup, built around singer Karen Matheson and accordion and keyboard player Donald Shaw, attracted a strong local following even in the early years. Capercaillie's reputation for tradition and innovation has grown in leaps and bounds since those formative days through commercially successful albums, work on soundtracks, and participation in a Hollywood movie (*Rob Roy*).

Get Out is a collection offering a good summary of Capercaillie through the 1980s and '90s and captures the energy of the band's live performances in several tracks. Also included is the recording that made history by being the first Gaelic song to chart in the U.K. Top 40, "Coisich a' Rùin," a haunting adaptation of a four-hundred-year-old waulking song.

In the past decade, Capercaillie's recordings began to utilize advanced production techniques as they explored other ethnic influences, such as the use of African rhythm. As a result, the band has pushed the boundaries of Gaelic song and Scottish instrumental music, blending these with pop and world influences. Through his creative vision and studio skills, accordionist and keyboard player Shaw has become a highly sought-after producer, helping to craft the cutting edge of Scottish music through work on many other artists' albums. His wife, Matheson, is one of the most prized vocalists in Scotland, and other Capercaillie band members, including flute player and uilleann piper Michael McGoldrick, bouzouki player and singer Mánus Lunny, fiddler Charlie McKerron, and bassist Ewan Vernal, all wield a significant influence in the Celtic music world.

Liz Carroll (b. 1956): Liz Carroll has won an international reputation as a master of Irish fiddle. Growing up in Chicago of Irish immigrant parentage, she became involved in the city's vibrant Irish music and dance scene at an early age. By the time she was in her teens, her musical appetite had taken her back to Ireland, where she scored victories in the All-Ireland fiddle championships. Mick Moloney included Carroll in his Green Fields of America concert tours during the 1980s, and the 1990s saw her working with accordionist Billy Mc-Comiskey and guitarist Dáthí Sproule in the critically acclaimed trio Trian.

Lost in the Loop (see Chapter 7, "Celtic Music on CD") is a fine example of Carroll's work, showcasing her skills as the accomplished composer of more than two hundred tunes, many of which have entered the traditional repertoire. Her superb writing ability, along with her outstanding command of her instrument, contributed to her citation as a National Heritage Award recipient by the National Endowment for the Arts in 1994, the highest award the United States can confer upon a traditional artist. The City of Chicago Mayor's office later added the tribute of naming a day in honor of their talented native daughter. Whether solo, in one of many duos, or appearing with a larger lineup (such as her involvement in the Celtic Connections festival's "String Sisters" project in 2000), Liz Carroll's performances—both live and recorded—exert an influence on Irish traditional music that is as exciting as it is far-reaching.

Karan Casey (b. 1972): Born in County Waterford, Ireland, Casey first came to prominence as lead singer with United States–based Solas, with whom she recorded and performed for several years from the mid-1990s. Concentrating upon her solo career since her 1997 debut *Songlines*, she is highly regarded for her clear, understated singing style and for her inspired choice of material. She sings with great empathy: Old songs are given a contemporary relevance, and newer compositions are invested with gravity and emotion.

On *Distant Shore*, Casey exhibits her ample interpretative skills with a deft selection of material from high-ranking songwriters, including Ewan MacColl, Billy Bragg, Matt McGinn, and Mary Brooksbank. A duet in Scots Gaelic with Karen Matheson is a special highlight. Casey found an ideal collaborator in Capercaillie's Donald Shaw, who produced the album. He drafted other Capercaillie alumni to contribute to the music, along with American Tim O'Brien on vocals and mandolin, and Casey's husband, concertina ace Niall Vallely.

Nollaig Casey (b. 1958): Fiddler Nollaig Casey is one of a celebrated musical family from Cork. Her sister, Maire Ni Chathasaigh, is a renowned harper. Nollaig studied violin at the Cork School of Music and later at University College, Cork. Often a disadvantage when approaching traditional music, she turned her classical training into an asset, applying brilliant technique to the music that was a permanent backdrop to her early years. As a result, she made an immediate impact on the traditional scene in the 1970s, while still finding time to play with the RTE Symphony Orchestra.

Lead the Knave and *Causeway*, Casey's two albums with playing partner and husband, Arty McGlynn, the first purely instrumental and the second also featuring Casey's fine singing, are considered masterpieces of Irish acoustic music (see Chapter 7, "Celtic Music on CD"). Guitarist McGlynn also works with Christy Moore, Paul Brady, Dónal Lunny, and Liam O'Flynn and is in great demand as a producer.

Ceolbeg (formed mid-1970s; disbanded 2002): When played on the bagpipes, the traditional dance music of Scotland (reels, jigs, hornpipes, and strathspeys) is known as *ceol beag*, literally "small music." This stands in contrast to *ceol mor*, or "big music"; the classical form of Scottish bagpipe music known as *piobaireachd* or *pibroch*. The band Ceolbeg took its name from the dance music form, but the repertoire and lineup of the band was very wide-ranging. Powerful bagpipes and delicate clarsach always combined at the core of Ceolbeg's instrumental sound. Although they may have seemed unlikely bedfellows, in the hands of Ceolbeg alumnae such as pipers Gary West and Mike Katz and percussive clarsach player Wendy Stewart, the pipes and harp always combined fluently and sat well amidst the flute, bouzouki, and keyboard mix.

From the beginning, Ceolbeg benefited from the involvement of especially strong singers such as the late Davy Steele and Rod Paterson, each regarded as an innovative interpreter of traditional and contemporary Scots song. In the early 1990s, an era when many groups were turning to keyboards for rhythmic reinforcement, Ceolbeg added a fully fledged drum and percussion kit, ably handled by pipe band drummer Jim Walker. This approach always guaranteed Ceolbeg a considerable impact on the concert stage.

An Unfair Dance showcases the powerful, expressive singing of Steele in traditional material and in his own songs, such as "The Collier's Way." Stewart's harp and West's pipes combine with flute, guitar, bouzouki, keyboards, and percussion, lending lift and lilt to the reels and jigs.

Cherish the Ladies (formed 1983): Together with New York's Ethnic Folk Arts Center, Irish musician and folklorist Mick Moloney produced a series of concerts in 1983 to highlight the remarkable contribution of young American women playing Irish traditional music. These performances were so well received that the National Endowment for the Arts funded an album featuring female singers and instrumentalists playing in solo, duo, and trio settings. Two of the women involved, flute player Joannie Madden and guitarist Mary Coogan, are still part of the permanent band that emerged from those concerts. Many lineup changes have only served to strengthen the sound and the commitment of this band, now beloved on both sides of the Atlantic for their outstanding musicianship and *joie de vivre*.

Before the *Riverdance* phenomenon, Cherish the Ladies were showcasing champion Irish step dancers in their performances and even on their recordings. Their dedication to this art has never wavered, even to the point of all the band members kicking up their heels in high-energy concert finales. *One and All: The Best of Cherish the Ladies* is a great introduction to the band's finest work through the late 1990s.

The Chieftains (formed 1963): Few bands, in any country's folk music, will be able to match The Chieftains for their impact, versatility, stability, and longevity. In the early 1960s, Irish music visionary Seán Ó Riada first brought together the traditional elements of Irish music in the folk ensemble Ceoltóirí Chualann: fiddles, concertina, flute, uilleann pipes, and bodhrán, with piano and harpsichord. The group included uilleann piper Paddy Moloney, who went on to form the earliest version of The Chieftains. Until the death of harper Derek Bell in 2002, the lineup of Bell and Moloney with Martin Fay and Sean Keane (fiddles), Matt Molloy (flute), and Kevin Conneff (bodhrán) as The Chieftains had remained unchanged for more than two and a half decades.

The band has circumnavigated the globe many times, scoring a number of firsts for Celtic music along the way. They won an Oscar; became the first Western group ever to play on the Great Wall of China; and collaborated with symphony orchestras, country stars, and rock legends. The Chieftains were also among the first to explore Ireland's shared musical roots with Brittany, Scotland, and Spain, championing such rising talents as the Galician piper Carlos Núñez. Their performance for the pope before an audience of 1.35 million in Dublin broke all attendance records for a live audience.

If you prefer your Chieftains pure, pick up *The Chieftains 10*, their 1981 album of mostly traditional Irish instrumentals. It finds the band at the height of their powers and in their pre-collaboration phase, just beginning to discover the links between Irish music and American standards such as "Cotton-Eyed Joe." On *Another Country*, collaborations run riot. With Chet Atkins, Willie Nelson, Emmylou Harris, Ricky Skaggs, Don Williams, and more, The Chieftains apply pipes, harp, fiddles, flute, whistle, and bodhrán to the Celtic-Country connection. The Chieftains' *The Long Black Veil* was certified gold in the United States, with sales in excess of half a million. It features collaborations with such artists as Mick Jagger, Sting, Van Morrison, and Sinéad O'Connor.

Clannad (formed 1968): This influential family-based group changed the sound of Celtic music and paved the way for the phenomenal success of sibling and onetime band member Enya. The origins of the band reveal a remarkable evolution in attitude toward traditional music and Irish song. After winning a contest and recording contract at the 1970 Letterkenny Folk Festival, Clannad's debut album stalled over their record company's discomfort with the use of Irish lyrics on the recording. Such a disagreement would be unthinkable in today's climate. Clannad won the argument and set a new trend in Celtic music.

The music of Clannad has evolved greatly since the early days when the siblings Máire, Ciaran, and Paul Brennan joined with their twin uncles Padraig and Noel Duggan to perform in the Brennan family pub in Donegal. Building upon the ethereal voice of Máire Brennan, Clannad initiated a fusion between Celtic, New Age, rock, and pop music. The popularity of the band reached unprecedented heights when "Theme from Harry's Game" charted in the U.K. Top 20 in the early 1980s and won *Billboard* Magazine's World Music Song of the Year award. It was later featured in the movie *Patriot Games*. Throughout their transition from traditional to contemporary music, Clannad continued to create lush, innovative productions, with Máire Brennan's singing and their use of Irish dance rhythms allowing them to keep faith with their Donegal roots.

In recent years, each of the members of Clannad has gone on to pursue solo work, most notably Máire, who received great critical acclaim for her solo debut, *Máire* (see Chapter 7, "Celtic Music on CD"), and her development of new music within the ancient traditions of Celtic Christianity. *Celtic Collections* samples from across Clannad's musical range and includes everything from simple ballads in Irish to the rock epic "In a Lifetime," featuring vocals from U2's Bono.

Cliar (formed 2000): This six-piece ensemble is based in the Highlands of Scotland and blends Gaelic song with traditional melodies and new writing from band members. Less well-known traditional material is infused with contemporary character. Central to the sound are the close harmony vocals of Arthur Cormack, Mary Ann Kennedy, and Maggie Macdonald, backed by an instrumental mix built around fiddle and clarsach. *Gun Tàmh—Restless*, winner of the Best Album award at the inaugural Scottish traditional music awards in 2003, is Gaelic music for the twenty-first century completely in touch with its ancient roots.

Tony Cuffe (1954–2001): From Greenock in the west of Scotland, this singer and guitarist's impact upon Scottish music will be as enduring as it is influential. After years of pioneering involvement with the traditional music scene in Scotland in Alba, Jock Tamson's Bairns, and Ossian, Tony settled near Boston in 1989. He then became established throughout the eastern United States as a popular solo performer and teacher, adding many instruments to his repertoire, including clarsach. Trawling old collections, he brought many lesser-known traditional Scottish songs into the limelight, sometimes arranging them with his own melodies. A fine example is "The Road to Drumlemman," which he recorded with Ossian on the album *Seal Song* (see Chapter 7, "Celtic Music on CD"), a timeless performance that gave the song its indelible identity. In his virtuoso guitar playing, he married tunes from pipe and fiddle traditions with contemporary guitar techniques and tunings to great effect and has influenced a generation of Scottish acoustic guitar players. *Sae Will We Yet* is a posthumous release and a gift to the many admirers of this uniquely talented musician; it comprises previously unreleased recordings gathered from private, concert, and studio recordings. Also included are love songs recorded by Tony Cuffe in the final months of his life.

John Cunningham (1957–2003): Johnny Cunningham first made his impact on the Scottish music scene through the music of Silly Wizard. With his brother Phil, Johnny and the band blazed a trail across Europe and North America, attracting a huge following for their music and legendary onstage antics. Key to their sound, and fueling the banter, was the fiddle and accordion duo of the Cunningham brothers. Silly Wizard front man and singer Andy M. Stewart remarked that their instrumental finger work was so fast and closely timed that only dogs could hear them.

After Silly Wizard disbanded, Johnny emigrated to the

United States, basing himself in Boston, where he worked as a musician and record producer. Shortly after the final Wizard tour, he was reunited with Phil in the unforgettable four-piece ensemble Relativity, which paired the brothers with Irish siblings Mícheál Ó Domhnaill and Tríona Ní Dhomhnaill. After two critically acclaimed albums in the mid-1980s, Johnny Cunningham and the Ó Domhnaills worked together again in the acoustic band Nightnoise, while Johnny explored another avenue for his fiddle in the rock band Raindogs. Cunningham also recorded *Fair Warning*, featuring uilleann piper Tim Britton and American guitarist Zan McLeod accompanying the fiddler in fiery reels and soothing slow airs.

On *The Celtic Fiddle Festival*, Cunningham teamed up with fiddlers Kevin Burke of Ireland and Christian LeMaître of Brittany for solo and group performances representing three proud Celtic heritages. With the backing of guitarist John McGann, each tune set shows off the dazzling individual technique of the players, highlighting his different styles and influences, while the collective sound is highly compatible and tremendously exciting.

Johnny Cunningham fronted an unforgettable gathering of Scottish fiddle players at the Smithsonian Folklife Festival in the summer of 2003. This was the last opportunity for many of his fans and musician friends to enjoy his great company and music before his sudden death at the end of that year.

Phil Cunningham (b. 1960): Although an outstanding keyboard and whistle player, Phil Cunningham is most revered for his exceptional abilities on piano accordion, and he has certainly done more to bolster the image of his instrument than any other individual. It was while he was a member of Silly Wizard in the 1970s and '80s that Cunningham started writing tunes. He now enjoys very high standing as a composer. The 1997 Celtic Connections Festival featured his specially commissioned "Highlands and Islands Suite," a major work for a seventy-three-piece orchestra, forty-strong choir, thirty Highland fiddlers, and other traditional players. *Airs and Graces*, Cunningham's first solo recording released more than two decades ago, is a classic. It reveals Cunningham's great gift as a composer and multi-instrumentalist, although it is on his signature accordion that he most obviously shines.

Phil Cunningham is in enormous demand as a record producer, working with artists from Scotland, Ireland, and the United States, and as a music director in the theater, writing instrumental music for award-winning stage productions. He has received numerous commissions for television and film and is often seen on the small screen performing with his longtime playing partner, the acclaimed Shetland fiddler Aly Bain.

Dáimh (formed late 1990s): The Scottish Highlands, Ireland, Cape Breton, and Irish America the origins of Dáimh's lineup speak volumes for Celtic music's international soul while the heart of Dáimh's attitude is revealed in the band's name, which is Gaelic for kinship or affinity. This fiery instrumental quintet employs rhythmic guitar and *bodhrán* to enhance pipes, fiddle, mandola, and banjo in tunes from band members' own traditions and beyond. *The Pirates of Puirt* followed their debut release and delighted a growing legion of Dáimh fans with a hot-blooded set of dance tunes and finely tuned slower melodies. Audiences worldwide have been thrilled by their particular brand of Celtic fusion, but these musicians make their way home after each tour to the West Highlands of Scotland where the musical community most inspires them.

De Dannan (also De Danann) (formed 1974): Formed in Spiddal, County Galway, this band is an Irish music institution. Membership in De Dannan has been a career springboard for some of today's best-loved Irish vocalists, including Dolores Keane, Maura O'Connell, Mary Black, and Eleanor Shanley. Fiddler Frankie Gavin and bouzouki player Alec Finn have been at the heart of the band through numerous lineup changes. Tired of common misspellings, they even changed the name to De Dannan along the way, mischievously using both this and the original spelling of De Danann on the first vinyl pressing of their 1987 album, *Ballroom,* just to create confusion (see Chapter 7, "Celtic Music on CD").

A virtuoso on fiddle and flute, Frankie Gavin is one of the most celebrated of the traditional Irish musicians. Together with Finn, Gavin is responsible for the driving instrumental arrangements and the eclectic repertoire for which the band is renowned. This includes a wide assortment of Irish material from the core of the tradition, from music hall, and from 1920s and '30s Irish American music. But it also ventures into gospel, klezmer, The Beatles, Bach, and the work of contemporary songwriters.

Song for Ireland is an unforgettable album for the involvement of vocalist Mary Black, especially on the title song, and for what was to be the first of several De Dannan arrangements of classical chestnuts. On this occasion it was to be Handel's "Arrival of the Queen of Sheba," from his oratorio "Solomon." With fiddle, button accordion, bouzouki, and bodhrán, Gavin and company transport the piece to Galway, where it fits in perfectly (although De Dannan's sound has been influential far beyond the shores of Galway). The future of the band is probably in question today, as the various members pursue individual projects, but De Dannan's position in the story of Irish music is secure.

Deaf Shepherd (formed mid-1990s; disbanded 2003): With pipes, twin fiddles, bouzouki, and bodhrán rallying behind the guitar and voice of singer John Morran, the members of Deaf Shepherd came from throughout Scotland. Their choice of material always reflected members' geographical sympathies, drawing in tunes and songs from the Borders to the Hebrides in a celebration of Scottish music. Their presence on the scene carried the tradition forward and attracted attention beyond their native shores, leading *Irish Music Magazine* to enthuse "you won't hear a better example of Scottish music." If you never saw this band live, *Even in the Rain* can at least take you there through the multimedia capabilities of a CD. It offers a video of Deaf Shepherd in concert, along with a full complement of great tunes and songs accessed the old-fashioned way.

Déanta (formed 1987; disbanded 1998): This Northern Irish band featured the instrumental strengths of the O'Briens: Kate on fiddle and viola and Eoghan on guitar and harp, although the riveting voice of All-Ireland champion vocalist Mary Dillon was central to the band's sound. Déanta's 1990 debut recording, *Ready for the Storm,* won them a following in the United States; however, they rarely toured because the band members were all part-timers with day jobs.

Dervish (formed 1988): The members of Dervish share a musical history that predates the formation of the band, having played together for years in Sligo's pub session scene. Even today, when they are not taking their music to appreciative fans throughout the world, there is a good chance you will find them playing in those same sessions. This background is obvious in the band's tight, animated instrumental sets, and their energetic playing draws upon momentum generated by such influences as The Bothy Band and De Dannan. Cathy Jordan provides stunning vocals around a core of fiddle, flute, and accordion, with mandola, bouzouki, and traditional percussion accompaniment. The combination clearly works; Dervish is one of the most respected and sought-after bands in today's Irish traditional scene. *Live in Palma* is a great introduction to the band with a double CD set of favorite songs and tune sets performed live in Palma, Majorca.

The Dubliners (formed 1962): The Dubliners forged their trademark rousing style in Dublin's O'Donoghue's Pub and emerged into the folk song revival of the early 1960s. Before long, they had scored an unlikely hit in the U.K. pop charts with "Seven Drunken Nights" in 1967. On the strength of this success, The Dubliners were on the road toward the legendary status they enjoy today. With the venerable Irish names and faces of Ronnie Drew, Luke Kelly, and the late Barney McKenna fronting the band, no other group has come close to matching them in their combination of Irish drinking songs, ballads, and bawdy material with genuine talent and authenticity.

30 Years a-Greying includes guest appearances from such luminaries as the Hothouse Flowers and Billy Connolly, which helps to make this an entertaining double CD collection, featuring the 1992 Dubliners lineup of Ronnie Drew, Barney McKenna, Eamonn Campbell, Sean Cannon, and John Sheahan. The band's 1987 duet of "The Irish Rover" with The Pogues was another massive hit. This ensured that the images and names of The Dubliners would live on in the hearts of a new generation of fans, while they hold ever true to the soul and humor that has sustained them through the decades.

The Easy Club (formed early 1980s): Named for an eighteenth-century Edinburgh drinking club, The Easy Club has made a unique contribution to what band member Jack Evans calls "the global ceilidh." The spirit of Django Reinhardt's "Hot Club" Jazz infuses the music of The Easy Club with the band applying a rhythmic approach to traditional tunes. The gaps between traditional music, jazz, and early acoustic rock 'n' roll have never been so successfully bridged.

Inspired by Duke Ellington's comment that only jazz and Scottish music swing, The Easy Club recorded *Scottish Rhythm and Swing* in 1984, following a successful appearance at the Edinburgh Folk Festival. Two more albums followed, consolidating a sound that combined the sublime voice and guitar of Rod Paterson, complimented by Jack Evans also on guitar, with cittern and percussion from Jim Sutherland, fiddle from John Martin (of Ossian and the Tannahill Weavers), and an early involvement of Norman Chalmers on concertina.

Rhythmic experimentation is not unusual at the progressive end of Celtic music, but The Easy Club also took the music in new harmonic directions and invented a sound that continues to inspire Scottish and Irish acoustic players.

Séamus Ennis (1919–1982): In the 1940s, the Irish Folklore Commission hired Séamus Ennis to travel throughout the west of Ireland, collecting songs and stories. He made the transition from folklorist and collector to broadcaster, working first for Radio Éireann and then the BBC in 1951. During this time he traveled throughout the British Isles and Ireland, gathering music for his radio program, *As I Roved Out*. His broadcasts introduced countless radio listeners to the authentic sounds of traditional music, recorded on location.

This pioneer of music radio is equally remembered as a

master uilleann piper, singer, and storyteller. *The Best of Irish Piping*, a two-CD set, combines Ennis's uilleann pipe recordings for the Tara label and features his remarkable epic performance of the tune "The Fox Chase." Ennis learned to play pipes from his father, James, and first recorded in the 1960s, bringing his music to the United States in a 1964 appearance at the Newport Folk Festival. By the time the revival of Irish folk music was in full swing in the 1970s, he was friend and mentor to piper Liam O'Flynn, who went on to play with Planxty. Ennis is revered today as one of the great names in Irish music.

Enya (b. 1961): Fans of the family-based Irish band Clannad who acquired a copy of their album *Fuaim* in 1982 could scarcely have imagined the phenomenal commercial success that the newest and youngest band member would find by the end of that decade.

Eithne Ni Bhraonain left Clannad to team up with producer Nicky Ryan and his wife, lyricist Roma Ryan, to compose film soundtracks and scores for BBC television. The trio used the phonetic spelling of Ni Bhraonain's first name, Enya, to brand a new sound building upon textures Ryan first explored with Clannad. Using piano and rich keyboard washes, they created a perfect soundscape for the central instrument of Enya's voice, working from a starting point of traditional Celtic song and elaborating into dreamy lyrics in Irish, English, Latin, and Spanish. The 1988 release of *Watermark* realized the full potential of Enya's musical influences, inspirations, and vision in the recording studio. The album sold more than four million copies and established Enya as an international artist. The mesmerizing combination entranced a worldwide audience, transported by the spiritual quality of Enya's music, the spellbinding vocal overdubs, and the fusion of ancient themes and New Age arrangements. As a result, Enya is the most successful Irish recording artist of all time.

Fine Friday (formed 2002): This combination of fiddle, flute, whistles, guitar, and vocals centers around the traditional trio of Anna-Wendy Stevenson, Kris Drever, and Nuala Kennedy of Edinburgh, Orkney, and Ireland. The band emerged from the Edinburgh session scene, playing regularly in the legendary folk pub Sandy Bell's. The trio has worked to retain the relaxed informality of these sessions, while honing a masterful concert set. Expressive, varied, and imaginative, *Mowing the Machar* built upon the success of Fine Friday's *Gone Dancing* debut.

Archie Fisher (b. 1939): From a well-known Glasgow singing family, Archie Fisher is highly respected as a songwriter and performer, often touring with English virtuoso guitarist John Renbourn and Canadian singer songwriter Garnet Rogers. He was a key figure in the Scottish folk song revival of the 1960s and '70s but is as well known in Scotland as a broadcaster, presenting the weekly program "Travelling Folk" for BBC Radio Scotland (see "Resources for Curious Listeners"). The program is an institution for followers of traditional and folk music in Scotland and beyond. Fisher also served as the director of the Edinburgh Folk Festival from 1988 to 1992.

Fisher was born into a singing household in the city of Glasgow. His Gaelic-speaking mother, father, and seven sisters were all singing partners in the early years, and with sister Ray he sang in a skiffle band in the early 1960s. The entire family participated in a 1965 release titled *The Fisher Family*, but it is as a solo artist that he went on to make his mark. *The Man with a Rhyme* showcases his signature guitar style and songs that have become classics in the Scottish folk repertoire. Some of these include "Men o' Worth," chronicling the changes brought about by the North Sea oil boom, and traditional-style ballads such as "Lindsay" and "The Witch of the West-mer-lands."

Cilla Fisher (b. 1952) and Artie Trezise (b. 1947): Along with her husband, Artie Trezise, Cilla Fisher followed in the footsteps of older brother Archie and made a strong impact as a folk singer early in her career. *Cilla & Artie*, released in 1979, was widely praised, winning "Folk Album of the Year" from the influential music publication *Melody Maker*. It is still considered a folk music classic. Since those days in the 1970s, the couple has entertained millions of children throughout the British Isles and beyond with their *Singing Kettle* theater performances, recordings (*The Best of the Singing Kettle*), television programs, and videos. In this way, they have introduced countless families to traditional Scottish children's play songs, adding many more of their own to this intergenerational repertoire.

Ray Fisher (b. 1942): Ray Fisher was a leading light of the Scottish folk song revival in the 1960s, who came under the wing of the legendary Jeannie Robertson early in her career. Robertson is regarded today as one of the richest sources of folk songs in living memory, and Fisher is recognized for her sincere, respectful approach to continuing this legacy. A genuine tradition-bearer, Fisher still performs on occasion with younger sister Cilla and brother Archie. Her *Traditional Songs of Scotland* is a prized collection enhanced by Colin Ross on Scottish small pipes and fiddle; John Kirkpatrick on button accordion, melodeon, and concertina; and guitar from the renowned English player Martin Carthy.

Alasdair Fraser (b. 1955): Originally from Clackmannan in Central Scotland, Fraser and his fiddle are a major musical force on both sides of the Atlantic. He has based himself in California for a number of years, where he directs the one hundred-member San Francisco Fiddlers orchestra and from where his Valley of the Moon fiddle school has inspired interest in Scottish fiddle styles all across North America. On frequent trips home to Scotland, Fraser has served as musician in residence at the Glasgow festival Celtic Connections and led hugely popular fiddle workshops from Edinburgh to the Isle of Skye.

Fraser is a great enthusiast of the authentic heritage of the Scottish fiddle and has been a vehicle for reconnecting Scottish fiddlers with the old Highland style of playing, preserved in Cape Breton, Nova Scotia. In 1988, he teamed up with American guitarist Jody Stecher to record *The Driven Bow*, a collection of Cape Breton and Scottish melodies. *Dawn Dance* is a refreshing and imaginative collection of all new music penned by Fraser. This recording won an INDIE Award for "Celtic Album of 1995."

Many Americans will know Alasdair Fraser for some particularly high-profile work. This includes his performances on movie soundtracks including *The Last of the Mohicans* and televised performances from the Kennedy Center and Lincoln Center, where he appeared with Itzhak Perlman. He has also won critical acclaim for his band Skyedance, which features piper Eric Rigler, wooden flute virtuoso Chris Norman, and keyboard player Paul Machlis. Skyedance plays mostly original music by Fraser and other band members.

Dick Gaughan (b. 1948): Born in Glasgow and raised in Edinburgh's port town of Leith, Dick Gaughan is one of the most respected acoustic guitarists and powerful singing voices in the United Kingdom. Early in his career, Dick was a member of Boys of the Lough and the folk-rock group Five Hand Reel, and in the intervening years, he has earned a formidable reputation as a solo performer. A voice for social justice, Gaughan is an articulate and passionate song interpreter and writer and has been an inspirational force within Scottish folk music circles since the 1970s. *Handful of Earth,* his 1981 album, was cited by many as the recording of the decade and included a moving performance of Burns's "Song for Autumn, Now Westlin' Winds" (see Chapter 7, "Celtic Music on CD"). A more recent double-CD anthology, *Prentice Piece,* features some of his most definitive work, including "Both Sides the Tweed" and "Flooers o' the Forest."

Had he never offered us his riveting singing and interpretative ability, Dick Gaughan would have captured our attention solely with his remarkable guitar playing. On his fretboard, traditional melodies are given a workout that retains all the character of their fiddle and pipe origins. He is a musical explorer on his instrument, offering breathtaking runs as he eases into the mood of a song. The 2004 Celtic Connections Festival in Glasgow culminated with the debut of Gaughan's long-anticipated "Guitar Concerto," a ninety-minute song cycle and instrumental suite.

Frankie Gavin (b. 1956): Like so many of Ireland's top traditional instrumentalists, Frankie Gavin was brought up in a musical family, living at the heart of a musical community. He took up tin whistle at age four, and at age seventeen, he won the All-Ireland Under-18 Fiddle and Flute titles. From an early age, he was also a regular in the session scene around Spiddal, County Galway, and quickly earned a reputation especially for his fiddle playing. His longtime playing partner, bouzouki specialist Alec Finn, was also part of that scene, and together they formed the famed band De Danann (later spelled De Dannan). The group first toured the United States in 1976 and has made countless return trips. Along the way, Gavin developed an interest in the 78-rpm recordings of Irish emigrants in the United States: James Morrison the Sligo fiddler, Galway piper Patsy Touhey, and the Flanagan Brothers have all provided inspiration for him.

Frankie Gavin 2003–2004 Collection is a four-album collection covering Gavin's career over the past decade and includes recordings of his performances with other outstanding instrumentalists, including his childhood friend, button accordionist Máirtin O'Connor, and the great jazz violinist Stephane Grappelli. The set includes live recordings of Gavin's phenomenal playing and conveys the camaraderie and musical accord he shares with his collaborators, especially with the late Grappelli during the Frenchman's two historic trips to meet Gavin in Galway. Gavin is a stunning solo player and is often called upon to perform during Irish State visits. Beyond his six solo albums, and the fifteen he made with De Dannan, Gavin and his fiddle have guested on many other artists' recordings, including The Rolling Stones and Earl Scruggs.

Martin Hayes (b. 1962): The fertile musical traditions of County Clare gave birth to this virtuoso fiddler, and he has extended his birthright in truly inventive ways. Hayes comes from a musical family in which his grandmother, father, and uncle all played traditional music. In moving to the United States in the 1980s, Hayes was exposed to a variety of styles and developed his own subtle elegant approach. The combination of his fiddle with the guitar of Chicago's Dennis Cahill offers a new level of musical interaction, where the instruments seem to combine and extend beyond their expected boundaries, and melodies are explored in depth. On *Martin Hayes and Dennis Cahill Live in Seattle*, captured in Seattle's intimate Tractor Tavern, the two-way interaction of artist and audience is palpable. Included is a remarkable medley lasting twenty-eight minutes, allowing the famed Hayes/Cahill musical dialogue to develop freely and extravagantly.

Joe Heaney (1919–1984): Growing up in Connemara among a family of singers and storytellers, Joe Heaney could hardly avoid absorbing a vast repertoire of songs. His father, Pádraig, was a cousin of one of Séamus Ennis's chief sources, a singer from whom the folklorist collected more than two hundred songs. Heaney first sang publicly in 1940 and was soon winning prizes at home before emigrating to Scotland in 1947, where he continued to sing. Eventually he drifted south to London and was swept up in the British Folk Revival of the 1950s and '60s, frequently performing at Ewan MacColl and A. L. Lloyd's "The Singers Club." He returned to Ireland and energized the Irish ballad boom of the early 1960s, along with Ronnie Drew and The Dubliners. In fact, it was Heaney who gave Ronnie Drew the song "Seven Drunken Nights," with which the Dubliners reached number one on the U.K. charts in 1967.

Hugely popular in the United States, folk singing group The Clancy Brothers invited Heaney to perform at the Newport Folk Festival of 1965, where he was very warmly received. He returned to the United States and settled in New York City a year later. In addition to performing, Heaney was eventually employed as a lecturer in Irish folklore, first at Wesleyan University, Connecticut, and by 1982 at the University of Washington in Seattle. In 1982, he was honored with a

National Heritage Award from the National Endowment for the Arts.

Throughout the American chapter of his life, Heaney continued to perform at festivals and concerts. He always held his audiences riveted by his dignified, powerful *sean nós* style singing, delivered at his particular pace and with careful, delicate ornamentation. With this unrivaled skill and his incredible repertoire of songs from Connemara and beyond, Heaney was an important cultural ambassador for Ireland and is often cited as the greatest *sean nós* singer in living memory.

Heaney's *The Road from Connemara,* a double-CD set, has everything for the enthusiast or student of Irish *sean nós* singing. Heaney stayed with Ewan MacColl and Peggy Seeger shortly before leaving for the United States and recorded a series of interviews with MacColl, together with more than forty songs and fragments. Thirty-three of these previously unissued recordings appear on this CD set, along with some of Heaney's introductions and explanations. The sixty-page booklet contains all the song words, along with a biography of Heaney and other essays.

Hamish Henderson (1919–2002): The life of Hamish Henderson was painted on an especially colorful canvas, and he ranks as one of the important cultural figures of twentieth-century Scotland. Henderson was a soldier and peace activist, who flourished as a poet, songwriter, collector and academic after his service during the Second World War. His extensive field work in the North East of Scotland helped to launch the fascinating and important recorded archive at the University of Edinburgh's School of Scottish Studies, and led to his discovery of ballad singer Jeannie Robertson, now celebrated as one of the leading figures in Scottish folk song. Henderson wrote extensively in Scots and his remarkable song "The Freedom Come All Ye" is often sung in his homeland as an alternative national anthem. In 1968, he arranged for The Corrie Folk Trio to record his song "Rivonia (Free Mandela)." A tape was smuggled on to Robben Island and heard by Nelson Mandela, who thanked Henderson in person years later.

Friends and admirers of Hamish Henderson gathered soon after his death to create *A' The Bairns O' Adam (Hamish Henderson Tribute)*, a collection of Henderson's songs and poems accompanied by extensive sleeve notes and song lyrics. The School of Scottish Studies song archive, which he helped establish, contributed three songs, including Henderson singing his own "51st Highland Division's Farewell to Sicily" and a field recording he made of Jeannie Robertson. Dick Gaughan, Adam McNaughtan, Rod Paterson, and Margaret Bennett are some of the artists who recorded songs and poetry especially for this collection, creating a fitting celebration of the great man's life.

Andy Irvine (b. 1942): This multi-instrumentalist and singer has been at the heart of evolving Irish music for more than four decades. Mandolin, bouzouki, and harmonica are all part of his venture, along with an unforgettable voice. Born in London, Irvine developed an early interest in the songs of Woodie Guthrie, a passion that still fuels his music today. In the 1960s, Irivine was involved in the Dublin traditional music scene and became part of the group Sweeney's Men, before leaving to travel extensively in Eastern Europe for many months. The rhythms and melodies of the Balkans still permeate his music, having first found their way to Ireland through Irvine's involvement with the highly influential Planxty in the early 1970s.

Andy Irvine called upon Bill Whelan to produce *East Wind* (with Davy Spillane), and with its eastern rhythms and instrumentation, it stands as an obvious forerunner to Whelan's *Riverdance*. In that respect, it was possibly ahead of its time, because it did not receive the attention it clearly deserved. Uilleann piper Spillane, pianist Mícheál O' Súilleabháin, and Hungarian folk music revivalist Márta Sebestyén all join Andy Irvine in this sensuous and enticing soundtrack.

Eileen Ivers (b. 1965): This Bronx-born artist is one of the most prodigious talents in all of Celtic music. Winner of nine All-Ireland fiddle titles and a tenth on tenor banjo, Ivers is a founding member of Cherish the Ladies and has toured as part of the original *Riverdance* ensemble. Her work with the London and Atlanta Symphony Orchestras, Patti Smith, the Hothouse Flowers, and Paddy Moloney of The Chieftains is an indication of Ivers's versatility, combining traditional artistry with the flair and authority she needs to mesh with other genres. She has appeared on more than eighty traditional and contemporary albums and created numerous movie scores.

Eileen Ivers is the daughter of Irish immigrants who exposed her to traditional music early on. At age eight, she began learning Irish fiddle from the legendary teacher Martin Mulvihill. However, it was as much the cultural diversity of her Bronx neighborhood that helped her create her signature sound. Now she balances her passion for tradition with her embrace of the rhythms of African, Latin, and American roots music. In 1999, she established a lineup that mixes African and Latin percussion and bass, Irish instrumentalists, and American blues vocals. *Eileen Ivers and Immigrant Soul* is true to the multicultural experience of Irish Americans while

remaining grounded in traditional Irish fiddle music. It real-
izes Ivers's dream of a "united nations of Irish music" with
moods ranging from the reverential to the raucous, steeped in
a multicultural marinade.

William (Billy) Jackson (b. 1955): Born in Cambuslang near Glasgow, Billy Jackson played for fourteen years with Ossian before embarking on a solo career, now combining this interest
with the re-formed band. As a composer, he derives inspiration from centuries of Scottish tradition, and his music incor-
porates images and landmarks from around the country.
Throughout his career, he has worked to overcome the boundaries between traditional and classical music and, in so do-
ing, he has developed a new style of Scottish music. During
his early Ossian years, the band was commissioned to write
music for a film about the island of Iona on the West Coast of
Scotland. The result was "Dove Across the Water," and it was
through this work that Billy Jackson began to realize the possibilities that lay in composing for classical and traditional instruments.

The west coast of Scotland continues as an inspiration in
Jackson's work. In 1996, The Scottish Chamber Orchestra
gave the first performance of his grand scale piece, "A Scottish Island," in which Jackson works with the sounds of the
Saltire String Quartet and the Kelvin Winds to evoke images
and elements of wild coastal seascapes. The Wellpark Suite
also drew inspiration from the west of the country, but for
this piece, Jackson traveled home to Glasgow. He was commissioned to write the music to celebrate the centenary of
Tennant's Lager, first brewed in Wellpark Brewery in May
1885. "The Wellpark Suite" brought together a wealth of
Scottish instrumental talent, all reunited for the ten-year

anniversary performance at Glasgow's annual Celtic Connections festival in 1995.

His native city also inspired the "St. Mungo Suite." This work featured The Scottish Orchestra of New Music, founded by Jackson as part of Glasgow's celebrations as Europe's Cultural Capital in 1990. One of the main instruments in this recording is the cello, and Jackson is quick to point out that the cello was long used in traditional music. Like other artists, including American cellists Abby Newton and Natalie Hoas, Billy Jackson is interested resurrecting the cello within traditional music.

In *Inchcolm*, Jackson journeyed to the other side of the mainland, deriving inspiration from an island on the east coast of Scotland (see Chapter 7, "Celtic Music on CD"). More than previous albums, *Inchcolm* allows spiritual undertones to come to the surface. "Salve Splendor," sung by Mae McKenna, is an arrangement of a chant from the thirteenth-century Inchcolm Antiphoner. This makes use of the authentic phrasing that monks on Iona would have used, connecting with his earlier composition "Dove Across the Water."

Jackson has been known as a composer of instrumental music, but "Land of Light" was written in response to a competition launched by *The Herald* newspaper, which began a search for "A Song for Scotland." This was prompted by a telephone poll of readers suggesting that many Scots wanted a new anthem to mark the re-establishment of a parliament in Edinburgh. There were 249 entries, but the judges were unanimous in selecting Jackson's "Land of Light" as the winner. Along the way, Billy Jackson became qualified as a music therapist and now divides his time between Scotland and Asheville, North Carolina. As for Ossian, the music continues with other longtime members still playing together on occasion, as other commitments allow.

Jock Tamson's Bairns (formed late 1970s): One of Scotland's most respected bands, Jock Tamson's Bairns were torchbearers for the revival in interest in traditional music in the late 1970s. The Bairns have fed members into many other influential groups, including Ossian, the Easy Club, Cauld Blast Orchestra, Ceolbeg, and the ceilidh band The Occasionals. The band still creates music on acoustic instruments only, avoiding synthesizers or digital sequencing. They have similarly sidestepped the fashion for importing elements of World Music percussion, relying upon the simple bodhràn to inject momentum into their dance tunes played on fiddles, whistles, guitar, harmonica, and concertina, all accompanying the singing of Rod Paterson. Their double CD, *A' Jock Tamson's Bairns,* includes the band's entire 1982 second album, *The Lasses Fashion,* and almost all of their self-titled 1980 debut release (see Chapter 7, "Celtic Music on CD"). These recordings were made at a time when Irish tunes were dominant in the Scottish traditional scene, yet the Bairns remained dedicated to the Scottish repertoire. They are among the most timeless albums in authentic Scottish traditional music, featuring brilliant singing and great imagination in the instrumentals and showing why Jock Tamson's Bairns became such a seminal force.

Dolores Keane (b. 1948): Born in Caherlistrane, County Galway, Dolores Keane grew up surrounded by traditional music and once remarked that "learning songs and tunes was like learning to walk." She benefited in particular from her aunts, Rita and Sarah, who are renowned for their rich heritage of Irish ballads. Keane was a neighbor of fiddle wizard Frankie Gavin, and he invited her to join the newly formed De Danann in 1974. She toured and recorded with the band for two years, joining them again a decade later for another two-year stint.

Keane's recordings with John Faulkner are Irish classics,

and her solo releases have spawned chart-topping singles in Ireland. *The Best of Dolores Keane* is a collection that draws from an extensive repertoire, including Keane's collaborations with Emmylou Harris, Mick Hanly, and De Dannan. The version of Lennon and McCartney's "Let It Be" is taken from De Dannan's *Anthem* and proves that, sung by Dolores Keane, any song is an Irish song. In the 1990s, she recorded with Emmylou Harris in Nashville for the BBC/RTE documentary *Bringing It All Back Home*, tracing the Irish influences in country music.

Kila (formed 1997): It didn't take long for this septet to be acclaimed as personifying the future of Irish music. Kila's sound fuses influences from Africa and the Caribbean with a foundation of Irish tradition and has caused reviewers to invent new labels such as "acid ceili," "Gaelic rap," and "trash trad." They generate a sense of tribal energy in their live concert sets and recordings, building dance grooves on traditional foundations. With the release of *Tóg é Bog é* (literally *Take It Easy*), the band really hit its stride. An inventive Irish take on a world ethnic vibe, *Tóg é Bog é* received a gold record for Irish sales.

Alison Kinnaird (b. 1949): Edinburgh-born Alison Kinnaird is internationally recognized as one of the leading players of the clarsach (Scottish harp) and is credited with leading the late-twentieth-century revival of her instrument. Winner of the harp competition at the Pan Celtic Festival in Killarney, she has also published three books on harp tunes and the history of the clarsach in Scotland (see "Resources for Curious Listeners"). She is a frequent partner to Gaelic singer Christine Primrose, has also collaborated with Battlefield Band, and is much sought after to teach at workshops.

The Harp Key, her first solo recording of clarsach, was turned down by record labels as being of little potential interest, inspiring Kinnaird and her husband, Robin Morton (a founding member of Boys of the Lough), to form their own label, Temple Records. This album quickly became a traditional music classic and helped to spark the contemporary worldwide interest in clarsach. Kinnaird is also Scotland's foremost glass sculptor and has recently developed ways to integrate her visual and musical arts. She created *Psalmsong*, a major music-inspired installation displayed at the Victoria and Albert Museum in London in 2004 involving glass, music, light, dichroic color, digital photography, and printed textiles. Her *Silver String* CD and DVD shows the relationship between Kinnaird's harp music and glass installations.

Kornog (formed 1981): In bringing together three instrumental virtuosos of traditional Breton music with a great Scottish ballad singer, Kornog found an unbeatable fusion of Celtic traditions: Soïg Siberil on guitar, Jean-Michel Veillon on flute and bombarde, and Christian Lemaitre on fiddle. Their sound is intermingled with the bouzouki and mandolin of Jamie McMenemy, who brings ballads from his native Scotland into the mix, setting them among the irresistible rhythms and melodies of Breton dance music.

In 1983, with *Première: Music from Brittany* (see Chapter 7, "Celtic Music on CD"), Kornog was the first Breton band to make an impact in the United States. Audiences were held spellbound by their exotic rhythms, masterly instrumental solos, and unique arrangements of Scottish songs. After taking a break in the 1990s, Kornog's winning coalition is finding new fans at festivals such as Glasgow's Celtic Connections.

Mary Jane Lamond (b. 1960): This Canadian singer possesses a remarkable voice and a talent that allows her to convey the emotion and depth of the traditional Gaelic songs she first heard when visiting her grandparents in Cape Breton. They inspired her to reclaim her heritage by studying Gaelic. She then went on to participate in the song tradition herself, reinvigorating it with her innovative arrangements and collaborations with the likes of fiddler Ashley MacIsaac.

Suas é! (literally *Go for It!*) is a sensual collection in which Lamont explores her Scots Gaelic inheritance while making a strong case that the traditions she upholds are part of a living culture in her Cape Breton home. Overlaid recordings of a spinning wheel and loom offset sophisticated studio production and contemporary arrangements. Lamond includes the voice of an elderly Cape Breton source singer and a chorus of friends at a home-styled milling frolic, while Ashley MacIsaac and Paul MacNeil add fiddle and pipes.

Lúnasa (formed 1997): Few bands have caused quite the stir created in recent years by Lúnasa. Named for an ancient Celtic harvest festival in honor of the god Lugh, patron of the arts, the five-piece lineup made an international impact shortly after releasing their debut album. Band members draw upon musical experiences with Sharon Shannon, Dónal Lunny, and *Riverdance*. Their pulsating instrumental sound relies upon the dialogue between pipes, fiddle, and flute in a Bothy Band–influenced repertoire of traditional tunes and new compositions. This mix of concert and studio tracks on *Lúnasa*, gathered from the first year of the band's life, was met with immediate acclaim, topping the Hot Press folk charts. *Folk Roots* (now *fROOTS*) magazine hailed it "a true must-have disc," and Lúnasa's reputation as one of today's foremost Irish music bands was sealed.

Dónal Lunny (b. 1947): Dónal Lunny is undoubtedly one of the most important figures in the history of Irish music. He was a founding member of three of its most influential bands—Planxty, The Bothy Band, and Moving Hearts. This would be impressive enough on most résumés, however Lunny has been at least as inspirational as a composer and record producer. The astounding list of production credits to his name includes Elvis Costello, Kate Bush, Rod Stewart, Christy Moore, Capercaillie, and Clannad.

Although the studio is now his preferred habitat, he is still very involved as a performing musician. Lunny uses mostly bouzouki and percussion to lead various innovative ensembles and musical projects through concert performances and television programs. For his first U.S. solo recording, *Coolfin*, Dónal Lunny called upon fiddler Nollaig Casey, uileann piper John McSherry, and accordion great Sharon Shannon to join his bouzouki, guitar, and keyboard work, while Hungarian folk diva Márta Sebestyén and Scotland's Eddi Reader added vocals. *Coolfin* was Lunny's turn-of-the-century musical statement and an album to return to with dividend.

Dónal Lunny is one of very few Celtic artists to have created a new, dynamic sound of his own, and he is hailed as the driving force behind much of the most cogent Irish music made today.

Ewan MacColl (1915–1989): Born in Auchterarder, Perthshire, this son of a Lowland Scots father and a Gaelic-speaking mother grew up in the industrial north of England. However, he inherited some of his parents' extensive song repertoire and their passion for the material. He became an influential author, playwright, actor, and leading voice in the folk song revival in England and Scotland, documenting folklife in numerous BBC broadcasts he called *Radio Ballads*. For these broadcasts, MacColl wrote many songs, including the classic "Shoals of Herring" from *Singing the Fishing* and "Thirty Foot Trailer" and "Go, Move, Shift" from *Travelling People*. MacColl was fascinated by the lives of the indigenous itinerant people of Scotland and developed a friendship in particular with the Traveling family, the Stewarts of Blair, from whom he collected many songs.

In the early days of his relationship with second wife Peggy Seeger (of the famed American singing family), MacColl wrote one of the most remarkable songs of the late twentieth century: "The First Time Ever I Saw Your Face." Singer Ray Fisher has said that MacColl "sang ballads amazingly, and when this was carried on from traditional songs to new songs he was writing you could scarcely tell the difference." Originally broadcast on BBC Radio 2, the recordings on *Folk on 2* were made at MacColl's seventieth birthday symposium in London and at the English Folk Dance and Song Awards, at which MacColl and his wife Peggy Seeger were presented with a gold medal.

Catriona Macdonald (*see* Blazin' Fiddles).

Maggie MacInnes (b. 1963): Maggie MacInnes has music in her blood, and the talent to make the most of her heritage. She is the daughter of Flora MacNeil, who has an unsurpassed knowledge of Gaelic song and is a generous font of material for many of today's singers. Naturally, the chief beneficiary is her daughter. All the songs on *Spiorad Beatha* (literally *The Spirit of Life*) were learned from MacNeil, who joins in the waulking song choruses along with her daughter and grandchildren. MacInnes's clarsach (Scottish harp) and voice are in rare form on the ancient Hebridean verses, accompanied by pipes, flute, keyboards, fiddle, saxophone, and guitars in various combinations. On voice and clarsach, MacInnes makes an impression far beyond the Hebridean homeland of her parentage. She has gained an international reputation with recordings of great authenticity and imagination.

Mairi MacInnes (b. 1964): In 1982, MacInnes became one of the youngest winners of the prestigious Gold Medal at the Mod, the annual competitive festival celebrating Gaelic language and culture. Since then, she has become a fixture on radio and television, most recently presenting children's programs, and releasing several albums of Gaelic song that have won international acclaim, particularly in Cape Breton, Wales, and Spain.

MacInnes was born and raised on the Hebridean island of South Uist, and the smaller island of Orosay, off the west coast, was a childhood haven. Her days there are remembered on *Orosay* with the voice of a five-year-old MacInnes included in the mix of one of the songs. Catherine-Ann MacPhee provides backup vocals, along with a host of luminaries, including Tony McManus on guitar, Billy Jackson on clarsach and whistles, and Iain MacInnes on small pipes.

Flora MacNeil (b. 1928): This highly acclaimed singer is often cited as the greatest living exponent of traditional Gaelic song. She emerged from an upbringing on the Island of Barra into the folk song revival of the 1950s and was the first Gaelic singer to take the songs of her culture to an international audience. Today, she is still a great ambassador for Gaelic language and song. MacNeil cannot remember when she first learned some of the age-old Gaelic songs featured on *Orain Floraidh— The Songs of Flora MacNeil.* They have probably been in her family for generations. She continues her distinguished legacy by inviting daughter Maggie MacInnes to join her on waulking song choruses and with clarsach.

Dougie MacLean (b. 1954): Dougie MacLean is a Scottish music pioneer. He was one of the first artists in the Celtic music world to use the droning Aboriginal digeridoo in his music. Early on in his career, he demonstrated the wisdom of retaining rights over the ownership of his songs. He is one of a select band of artists to develop a state-of-the-art home-based digital studio for producing his own recordings. He launched a website in the early days of the Internet and went on to trailblaze web-based projects, including producing a live web concert and an mp3 download of one of his songs. New projects blossom with each passing season, yet it is for one of his earliest compositions, the 1977 anthem "Caledonia," that he is internationally renowned (see Chapter 6: "The Music").

MacLean began his remarkable international travels as fiddler with the Tannahill Weavers in the 1970s. After a brief spell with Silly Wizard in the early 1980s, he embarked upon his career as a singer songwriter and primarily as a solo performer, and it is in this way that he built his international reputation as a songwriter. He has taken his music to concert stages and festivals all over the world, including Carnegie Hall in New York. Irish artists Mary Black, Dolores Keane, and Deanta, and U.S. country singer Kathy Mattea number among the singers to have covered his songs. His music has been used in television dramas and Hollywood films, including *Last of the Mohicans*, and he has been the subject of BBC television documentaries. *The Scotsman* newspaper has called him "a performer of extraordinary warmth and ease."

Along with his artist wife, Jennifer, MacLean runs Dunkeld Records, an independent record label, recording studio, and publishing company. Whether singing about land politics, the environment, history, or relationships, MacLean's music and work practices are infused with a tangible sense of place. In *Perthshire Amber*, he created a large-scale work for Scottish traditional musicians and string ensemble, celebrating the seasons and landscapes of his native county.

Buddy MacMaster (b. 1924): Hugh Allan "Buddy" MacMaster is an inspirational force for Cape Breton music. The fiddler from Judique has inspired many young musicians to follow in his stead, including his niece Natalie. MacMaster was born into a Gaelic-speaking household, and he soon developed a reputation as a fine player with a vast repertoire of traditional Scottish fiddle music. An employee of the Canadian National Railroad until his 1988 retirement, he would often practice his fiddle at work between train arrivals and departures. On *The Judique Flyer*, MacMaster's friends and family members (some of the best Cape Breton pianists) partner the fiddler in this celebration of his music and the venerated Cape Breton style. In 2003, MacMaster received the Order of Nova Scotia, the highest honor of the Province, for helping to preserve the Celtic Culture of his homeland.

Natalie MacMaster (b. 1972): Niece of the legendary fiddler Buddy MacMaster, Natalie clearly inherited the family talent for the instrument and has made a huge impact on the international world and roots music scenes. Her driven rhythm, brilliant technical ability, and wonderful Cape Breton repertoire have made her a festival favorite on both sides of the Atlantic. She is also celebrated for her ability to step dance while playing. This conveys something of the joy her music gives her and her audiences in equal measure, palpable on her electrifying double-CD release *Natalie MacMaster Live* (see Chapter 7, "Celtic Music on CD").

James Malcom (see Old Blind Dogs).

Malinky (formed 1998): Maintaining an acoustic approach to the music, Malinky offers one of the most distinctive Scottish sounds of the present era. Among the lineup, Karine Polwart offered striking vocals, representing a new generation of singers performing and writing new old-style songs in Scots. Her contemporary writer's voice speaks to the Scottish experience past and present, while celebrating the ancient form of the narrative ballad. On *3 Ravens,* innovation met tradition as Polwart and other band members, including button box player Leo McCann wove their own work among the ancestral fabric. This accomplished collection of songs and instrumentals include Polwart's award-winning ballad "Thaney," hewn in rich Scots dialect. In 2004, Polwart left Malinky to pursue an opportunity as a songwriter.

Karen Matheson (see Capercaillie).

John McCusker (b. 1973): John McCusker was raised among the ceilidh bands and youth orchestras of Glasgow, and he formed the group Parcel o' Rogues while still in his early teens. By age sixteen, he had accepted an invitation to join the renowned Battlefield Band, with whom he toured the world for eleven years. During this time, he perfected his prodigious skills on fiddle while developing his command on a range of instruments, including whistles, piano, and cittern.

Since leaving Battlefield Band to develop his solo career, McCusker has guested on countless albums by pop, rock, country, and traditional artists, in addition to cultivating a career as producer of some of the most critically acclaimed acoustic roots, folk, and traditional albums of recent years.

McCusker's work on his wife Kate Rusby's release *Sleepless* was rewarded with a Mercury Music Prize nomination in 1999, and 2003 saw the release of the Damien O'Donnel movie *Heartlands*, featuring his soundtrack. All this is in addition to an abundance of original John McCusker tunes unveiled in the course of his own highly praised albums. For *Goodnight Ginger*, McCusker invited a succession of music pals to his home, developed tunes in the informal sessions that transpired, and recorded them in his own studio next door. The pals included guitarists Ian Carr and John Doyle, accordionists Andy Cutting and Phil Cunningham, with Michael McGoldrick and Iain MacDonald on flute and pipes. Kate Rusby contributed a vocal track. The result is not to be missed. McCusker is undeniably one of the busiest of all Celtic musicians, and for his outstanding contribution to Scottish cultural life, he was presented with the Spirit of Scotland Award for Music in 2000.

Arty McGlynn (b. 1944): Arty McGlynn's reputation for guitar artistry has traveled far beyond his birthplace of Omagh, County Tyrone. He first started playing guitar at age eleven and began to delve into the music of jazz guitarists Wes Montgomery and Barney Kessel. By age fifteen, he was playing professionally. Within the space of a few short years, beginning with a spell in Paul Brady's band, he toured the world with Van Morrison, Maura O'Connell, Makem and Clancy, Andy Irvine, Planxty, and Patrick Street.

McGlynn and his playing partner and wife, fiddler Nollaig Casey, recorded two superb albums with *Lead the Knave* and *Causeway* (see Chapter 7, "Celtic Music on CD"). The first purely instrumental and the second featuring Casey's fine singing, each is considered a masterpiece of Irish acoustic music. McGlynn also plays and records with Christy Moore, Paul Brady, Dónal Lunny, and Liam O'Flynn. In demand as a producer, he has won acclaim for his work on recordings by Four Men and a Dog, Christy Hennessy, and Francis Black.

Michael McGoldrick (b. 1971): Born and raised in England, Mc-Goldrick is fully connected to his Irish cultural roots and has dazzled audiences on flute, whistle, and uilleann pipes, all now valued elements in the sound of Capercaillie. He sits at the innovative edge of Celtic music, drawing influences from jazz, world music, and hip hop into his work. In *Fused,* he surrounded himself with a dazzling assortment of musicians from the British Isles and Ireland to make for an exciting album (see Chapter 7, "Celtic Music on CD").

Loreena McKennitt (b. 1957): Canadian Loreena McKennitt got her start in folk clubs. Her career in music was fully launched at the Shakespeare Festival in Stratford, Ontario, where she sang, composed, and acted. These experiences fueled her interest in setting the words of Blake, Yeats, and Tennyson to music, and it wasn't long before she was developing her own sound around her transcendental, emotion-filled voice and harp playing. Inspired by Celtic and other folk elements, McKennitt strives for a spiritual dimension in her composing and is increasingly swept up in a quest to investigate the common undercurrents in indigenous music from various lands. Her albums are rich productions indeed, layering a variety of ethnic instruments into a commercial sound that has won her a phenomenal international following. Her "Mummer's Song" gained a great deal of crossover radio airplay in 1997. *Live in Paris and Toronto* documented McKennitt's live experience in these cities during a three-month tour of Europe and North

America. Her harp, piano, keyboards, accordion, and mezmerising voice are given the backing of a largely acoustic eight-piece band. Fans of McKennitt will find all their favorite titles here, and the satisfaction of knowing that these live performances were left unaltered when the tapes arrived at the studio, making the achievement all the more impressive.

Tony McManus (b. 1965): Self-taught Scottish guitar wizard McManus has developed a solo guitar repertoire of startling originality, combining a fiendishly dextrous technique with a deep love of traditional music of the islands of his homeland and beyond. In addition to drawing upon the traditions of the Celtic diaspora, he is well versed in the music of Quebec and Eastern Europe, and in jazz techniques.

On *Ceol More,* McManus uses Scotland as a starting place for a musical expedition to Ireland, Brittany, North America, and Central Europe; his spectacular guitar playing unifies the disparate influences. McManus is also able to bring an element to guitar playing that few before him have achieved, an ability to ornament tunes with the same passion that most would associate with the fiddle, accordion, or bagpipes. Besides other instrumental influences, the haunting art of Gaelic song has touched his playing, and he is able to translate, on guitar, the powerful emotions these songs evoke. Vocalists such as Mairi MacInnes appreciate his sensitive, imaginative accompaniment, and he can be heard on hers and other Gaelic artists' recordings.

Brian McNeill (b. 1950): Devotees of the Scottish music scene over the last few decades often venerate it as a "living tradition." Traditions in song and instrumental music are shaped and developed by people at ease with their heritage, and new writing courses through the veins of the music. Multi-instrumentalist, singer songwriter, and teacher Brian Mc-Neill is moved to work with Scottish musical traditions in all these ways, but it's as a composer that he's made his most significant contributions.

McNeill launched his body of work during years with the seminal Battlefield Band, which he co-founded. Since leaving in 1990, he has written an immense number of tunes and songs and inspires young musicians to do the same in his work as director of the Traditional Music program at the Royal Scottish Academy of Music and Drama in Glasgow.

In 1991, he released *The Back o' the North Wind*, a cycle of songs telling the tales of individual Scottish immigrants to North America. This album underscores McNeill's great storyteller's gift as he spins his tales. Apart from the fine writing and the impressive roster of backing artists, including Dick Gaughan (guitar and vocals) and Dougie Pincock (pipes, whistles, and saxophone), this album parades McNeill's peerless instrumental abilities on fiddle, guitar, bouzouki, mandocello, hurdy-gurdy, concertina, and bass. His interest in history and storytelling has led him through the production of another anthology. *Baltic to Byzantium* chronicles mostly unknown stories of the Scots in Europe, and this musical globe-trotting takes him to Africa next. McNeill is also a published author of novels featuring, as the central character, a busking fiddler.

Matt Molloy (b. 1947): Wooden flute player Matt Molloy first rose to prominence in the 1970s as a member of two pivotal Irish groups: Planxty and The Bothy Band. He learned to play from his father and won the All-Ireland title while still in his teens. Molloy joined The Chieftains in 1979 and has toured the world with the legendary ensemble, an ideal showcase for his exceptional talent. Apart from appearing on Chieftains albums, Molloy has recorded solo (including *Stony Steps*, see Chapter 7, "Celtic Music on CD") and in the company of other well-known Irish instrumentalists. When at home, he can sometimes be heard playing music for fun in his own pub, Matt Molloy's, in Westport, County Mayo.

Mick Moloney (b. 1944): This string player is renowned for his brilliant technique on tenor banjo and is also an expert mandolin player, guitarist, and singer who was involved in some of Ireland's popular 1960s folk bands, Emmet Folk and The Johnstons. He emigrated to the United States in the early 1970s to pursue a Ph.D. in folklore at the University of Pennsylvania. Since then, he has dedicated himself to uncovering, documenting, and nurturing Irish American music, forming such bands as The Green Fields of America and Cherish the Ladies, organizing festivals, and encouraging outstanding younger players such as Seamus Egan of Solas. Moloney also leads summer tours to Ireland to give American visitors a chance to encounter authentic Irish traditional music in its natural habitat.

On *The Green Fields of America: Live in Concert*, Moloney's Irish American lineup of the late 1980s featured Moloney with Robbie O'Connell, Jimmy Keane, Seamus Egan, Eileen Ivers, and step dancers Donny and Eileen Golden. Highlights of this live performance include the moving immigration ballad, "Kilkelly," and a medley played in tribute to the prolific Irish traditional musician and composer Ed Reavy.

Christy Moore (b. 1945): This man is truly a giant of Irish folk music. His 1972 album *Prosperous* was the spark that ignited the formation of the highly influential traditional band

Planxty, with whom Moore played for two years. A decade later, he helped create Moving Hearts, another trailblazing band combining traditional instrumentalists with saxophone, keyboards, and drums in high-energy rock arrangements. Along the way, Moore has sharpened his skills as a singer songwriter, emerging as voice for social and humanitarian concerns with songs such as "Ordinary Man." That song is one of the many great Christy Moore titles included on *The Christy Moore Collection 1981–1991*, which draws upon the output of a memorable decade in the singer songwriter's career.

Hamish Moore (b. 1950): Hamish Moore has received international acclaim for restoring and generating interest in the bellows-blown bagpipes of Scotland. Also known as cauld wind pipes, this group of instruments includes the Scottish small pipes, the lowland pipes, and the pastoral pipes. Cauld wind pipes refers to the temperature of the air in the bellows in contrast to the warmer breath of the mouth-blown pipes.

Moore grew up with an interest in piping encouraged by his father, who played the Highland pipes. Progressing on through formal piping training at school, his expertise was evident early, and he won many championships in solo piping and as a pipe band member. However, his chosen vocation was not music but veterinary medicine, and Moore spent several years working as a vet in the Scottish Highlands.

A chance event in 1981 renewed and changed Moore's musical interests and the direction of his career. A friend lent him some nineteenth-century Scottish small pipes and lowland pipes that his father had collected. These bellows-blown instruments had rarely been heard since the end of that era, though up until then they had often been used as accompaniment at dances and festivals. Moore became very interested in collecting, restoring, and playing these nearly extinct instruments. In fact, his work with the pipes became so all-encompassing that he eventually decided to give up his practice as a veterinary surgeon to devote time to recording, promoting, and building Scottish bellows-blown pipes.

Moore's pipe-making business has since grown to include his son, piper Fin Moore, and their handmade instruments are heard played throughout the world. Father and son are also in demand as teachers of lowland and small pipes, and they have led workshops in Scotland, the United States, and Canada. On *Farewell to Decorum*, acclaimed saxophonist Dick Lee and other jazz players join Hamish Moore for an unusual collection of jazz-flavored traditional tunes.

Moving Hearts (formed 1981; disbanded 1985): The parameters of Irish music were redefined by this band's fusion of rock, jazz, and Celtic passion. With Dónal Lunny and initially Christy Moore at the hub, the group combined traditional instruments, including Davy Spillane's uilleann pipes, with saxophone, keyboards, electric guitar, and drums, and laid new pathways that roots-influenced rock bands have followed ever since. Some would consider a Celtic music record collection incomplete if it failed to display a copy of Moving Hearts' *The Storm* (see Chapter 7, "Celtic Music on CD").

Maire Ni Chathasaigh (b. 1956): Ni Chathasaigh was born into a musical family and started playing harp at age twelve. She is now hailed as Ireland's most innovative harper. Ni Chathasaigh was the first Irish harper to infuse her playing with the techniques of traditional ornamentation, commonly practiced by fiddlers and pipers, and she recast the harp as an instrument fully capable of handling the dance idiom. She is the sister of fiddler Nollaig Casey and runs her own record label,

Old Bridge Records. In partnership with the accomplished guitarist Chris Newman, she can work her way through jazz, American flat-picking tunes, and Irish dance music with ease. On *The Carolan Albums*, she tackles the repertoire of the great seventeenth-century Irish bard Turlough O'Carolan on every instrument imaginable. With her technically brilliant playing, Ni Chathasaigh's compilation is a must for anyone interested in hearing O'Carolan's compositions on his chosen instrument.

Mícheál Ó Domhnaill (*see* The Bothy Band, Kevin Burke, John Cunningham, Nightnoise).

Tríona Ní Dhomhnaill (*see* The Bothy Band, John Cunningham, Nightnoise, Chapter 7, "Celtic Music on CD").

Nightnoise (formed 1983; disbanded 1998): This band began as a duo of Mícheál Ó Domhnaill on guitar and Billy Oskay on violin. By the late 1990s, they had been recording and touring as a quartet, including singer and keyboard specialist Tríona Ní Dhomhnaill, fiddler Johnny Cunningham, and flute player Brian Dunning, with Ó Domhnaill a constant presence on guitar. Nightnoise was quickly categorized as "New Age"; however, their music was always more rooted than many similarly labeled offerings and benefited from the considerable asset of Ní Dhomhnaill as songwriter and singer. *A Different Shore* includes a blend of flute, fiddle, guitar, and piano, and Ní Dhomhnaill's peerless Irish singing pitches the band's new acoustic and contemporary Celtic arrangements at a perfect balance with traditionally flavored material. Sometimes called "chamber folk," the music of Nightnoise bore influences of classical and Celtic music, and almost always incorporated traditional themes and impressions.

Carlos Núñez (b. 1972): This dazzling performer is a virtuoso on the gaita, Galician bagpipes, and also on recorder and whistle. Trained in Baroque music at the Madrid Conservatory, at age twelve he enthralled The Chieftains' Paddy Moloney with his playing. His work with The Chieftains on their album *Santiago* highlighted the cultural links between Ireland and Spain, helping to draw the world's attention toward the Northwestern Spanish region of Galicia, once dubbed "the undiscovered Celtic country." Today, Núñez is Galicia's most celebrated champion. With his blend of exhilarating dance tunes and soulful melodies, he has been a key player in the revival of Spanish Celtic music. Most recently, his musical interests have helped create a bridge between Celtic and Flamenco music and followed pathways into fado, gypsy, North African, and Cuban styles.

Dónal Lunny, Derek Bell, Liam O'Flynn, Dan Ar Braz, Frankie Gavin, Phil Cunningham, Sharon Shannon, and Mike Scott of the Waterboys is but a partial list of the Pan-Celtic convention surrounding Núñez on *Os Amores Libres* for this merging of Galician melody, flamenco rhythm, and gypsy passion. With Jackson Browne, Hector Zazou, and Vincente Amigo also appearing, this truly is World Music.

Maura O'Connell (b. 1958): Although Maura O'Connell originally hails from the town of Ennis, County Clare, in the West of Ireland, a region rich with traditional songs and tunes, the bearer of one of Ireland's most distinctive voices has lived in Nashville for many years.

Publications ranging from *The Washington Post* to *Cosmopolitan* have admired O'Connell's memorable interpretations and stylish taste in songs. The singer selects material from among the best traditional and contemporary composers, including Karla Bonoff, Nanci Griffith, Eric Clapton,

Patty Griffin, Tom Waits, Shawn Colvin, Mary Chapin Carpenter, and Linda Thompson. Yet if she followed the path she planned, she'd be a fishmonger.

Born into a musical family, O'Connell expected to take over the family fish shop started by her grandmother and perform on weekends for friends and neighbors, as her mother and sisters did. Members of De Dannan (then De Danann) happened to hear one of her shows and invited her to join the group on a six-week U.S. tour. Her gradual appreciation for traditional sounds, along with the chance to see America, eventually persuaded her to go. With O'Connell as lead singer, the band recorded *Star Spangled Molly*, De Dannan's most successful album ever and one that spawned two Irish hit singles. She ended up staying with De Dannan two years before going solo. In 1987, she began a new phase of her musical life in the acoustic music scene of Nashville, releasing her U.S. debut *Just in Time* in 1988, and *Helpless Heart* the following year, which was nominated for a contemporary folk Grammy. O'Connell contributed a contemporary sound to the hugely successful albums *A Woman's Heart* and *A Woman's Heart 2*.

After several releases, Maura O'Connell returned to Irish songs for 1997's *Wandering Home*. This selection of traditional songs and new writing reunited O'Connell with the best of Ireland's string players, and John McSherry's uilleann pipes and whistle grounded a couple of the songs. At home with the Celts, Jerry Douglas uses his dobro to keep the Nashville connection intact in *Wandering Home*. In Nashville, Maura O'Connell continues to make guest appearances on other artists' albums, including Dolly Parton, Van Morrison, and Rosanne Cash, and to make music with longtime collaborators Jerry Douglas, Bela Fleck, and Tim O'Brien.

Liam O'Flynn (b. 1950): O'Flynn was born into a musical family in county Kildare surrounded by some outstanding pipers who nurtured his early playing. Today he is widely regarded as one of today's foremost uilleann pipers, having co-formed the legendary Irish band Planxty and contributed to such groundbreaking projects as Shaun Davey's *Brendan Voyage*, in which O'Flynn played the demanding solo parts (see Chapter 7, "Celtic Music on CD"). On *The Fire Aflame*, O'Flynn collaborated with The Chieftains' Sean Keane (fiddle) and Matt Molloy (flute) to create an instrumental all-star trio, with guitar ace Arty McGlynn providing backing.

Old Blind Dogs (formed 1990): Aberdeenshire in the Northeast of Scotland is a hotbed of fiddle music and home to many a great ballad singer. Old Blind Dogs came together in that particular musical environment and have breathed new life into many of the standard tunes and songs of the region. From the outset, the band incorporated Afro Caribbean–style hand percussion, and this unlocks new rhythmic possibilities in the fiddle and pipe music while seasoning the singing. Folk song veteran Ian Benzie provided the lead vocals for much of the band's first decade, along with fellow founding members fiddler Jonny Hardie and Buzzby McMillan on bass and cittern. The voice of Old Blind Dogs is currently James Malcolm from the Angus area of Scotland. Tinted with blues and jazz hues, Malcolm possesses one of the warmest voices in Scottish music and is developing a reputation as a songwriter and guitarist of substance. *The World's Room* is a particularly strong selection of tunes and songs from this most respected band, including concert favorites "Forfar Sodger" and "Edward." The arrangements are progressive and dramatic from a lineup supported by Rory Campbell on whistle, border pipes, and vocals.

Seán Ó Riada (1931–1971): In the 1950s, Ó Riada was musical director of Dublin's Abbey Theatre. He used his position to promote the use of Irish traditional music at a time when the appreciation of these musical styles was restricted mostly to rural Ireland. He also created orchestral music and film scores that brought traditional sounds, for the first time, into the consciousness of the majority of the Irish people. In the early 1960s, Ó Riada combined the traditional elements of Irish music in the first Irish folk ensemble, Ceoltóirí Chualann, featuring fiddles, concertina, flute, uilleann pipes, and bodhrán, with Ó Riada on piano and harpsichord. The group rediscovered the music of Carolan to parent the earliest lineup of The Chieftains. *Ó Riada's Farewell*, a traditional selection including Carolan compositions, is Ó Riada's lasting bequest. It was recorded only two months before his sudden death at the young age of forty and is one of only a few performances of Irish music on harpsichord.

Mícheal Ó Súilleabháin (b. 1950): Straddling the European classical and Irish traditions, this consummate pianist from County Tipperary is also a composer, lecturer, and broadcaster. He studied music in the National University of Ireland, Cork, and at Queen's University, Belfast, and was appointed lecturer in music at University College Cork in 1975. Ó Súilleabháin was already recording by then, but it was his 1987 release, *The Dolphin's Way*, that captured the attention of music fans and critics. His piano improvisations around Irish themes bridged traditional, jazz, and classical music in a style reminiscent of the work of jazz pianist Keith Jarrett.

Since his debut, Ó Súilleabháin has collaborated increasingly with the Irish Chamber Orchestra, setting traditional instrumentalists in its midst and integrating the two styles to excellent effect. He used this synthesis in his acclaimed soundtrack for the classic silent movie *Irish Destiny*. For the ensemble work on *Oileán/Island*, Ó Súilleabháin placed traditional musicians Matt Molloy (flute), Mel Mercier (bones), Colm Murphy (bodhrán), and Tony McMahon (button accordion) against the orchestral backdrop and used his piano to unify the elements of both traditions in music of rare eloquence.

In 1994, upon his appointment as the first Chair of Music at the University of Limerick, Ó Súilleabháin established the Irish World Music Centre. Four years earlier, while completing a semester as Visiting Professor at Boston College, he founded the Archive for Irish Traditional Music in America. Ó Súilleabháin often works within the media of film, radio, and television. He devised, scripted, and presented the landmark television series on Irish music, *A River of Sound*, in association with RTÉ and the BBC (see Chapter 7, "Celtic Music on CD").

Ossian (formed 1976): In the 1970s and '80s, the name of Ossian was synonymous with the best in Scots and Gaelic song and richly textured harp, pipes, and fiddle instrumentals. Few bands managed to approach the benchmark set by Ossian in counterbalancing sensitivity and power so effectively, as they blended harp; fiddle; whistles; uilleann, Highland, and small pipes with an array of stringed instruments. The re-launch of Ossian in 1997 insures that this direction carries on into the twenty-first century. Founding members Billy Jackson and Billy Ross have been important figures in Scottish music. Their multiinstrumental involvement, with the Gaelic and Scots vocals of Ross, continues in the present lineup. Ossian is also remembered for the enduring work of the late George Jackson and the late Tony Cuffe. *Seal Song* is one of the band's seminal recordings (see Chapter 7, "Celtic Music on CD").

Niamh Parsons (b. 1958): This talented singer from Dublin works with English-language songs from the Irish tradition, deftly handling the epic ballads alongside work by a new generation of Irish composers. In the mid-1990s, she performed and recorded as part of the well-regarded group Arcady, but has been most praised for her solo albums where her rich vocals take center stage. On *Blackbirds and Thrushes*, the material is strong and Parson's delivery highly persuasive. The album includes a definitive version of the old Scots Gaelic song, "Fear a Bhata" ("The Boatman").

Rod Paterson (b. 1953): Today's leading interpreter of the songs of Robert Burns, Rod Paterson was an important member of the team that created the definitive Burns anthology on Linn Records. He has also contributed to the sound of some of Scotland's best-known traditional bands, including Jock Tamson's Bairns, The Easy Club, and Ceolbeg. Whether working with traditional material or his own songs, Paterson blends Scots- and jazz-style vocals, the jazz influence also flavoring his guitar and mandola playing. On *Songs from the Bottom Drawer*, Scotland's great interpreter of Robert Burns songs has brought together musicians from Ceolbeg, Battlefield Band, The Easy Club, and Jock Tamson's Bairns to assist him in this project. Familiar and obscure songs of Burns are included, none of which Paterson had committed to record before.

In addition to his career in mostly traditional music, Paterson has always been in demand for stage and television productions, working with such artists as Phil Cunningham, Emmylou Harris, and Eddi Reader.

Patrick Street (formed 1986): Patrick Street was conceived as an all-star Irish lineup, involving Andy Irvine (vocals, bouzouki, mandolin), Kevin Burke (fiddle), Jackie Daly (button accordion), and guitarist Arty McGlynn, who played with the band until 1994. Ged Foley from the northeast of England replaced McGlynn on guitar and has added Northumbrian pipes to Irvine's song repertoire and the inventive dance tune medleys. Patrick Street doubled the size of the lineup for the recording of *Irish Times,* bringing Bill Whelan (of *Riverdance*) on keyboards, piper Declan Masterson, guitarist Gerry O'Beirne, and fiddler James Kelly into the fold. This pays off especially on the instrumentals, including a definitive version of "Music for a Found Harmonium" (see Chapter 6, "The Music"). Although all the band members are involved in a wide variety of other projects, Patrick Street has enjoyed considerable longevity, remaining a favorite at Celtic music festivals throughout the world.

Planxty (formed 1972; disbanded 1983): In 1972, Irish singer Christy Moore was preparing to record his debut album at Downing's Pub in Prosperous. He had only just returned to Ireland after time spent touring on the English folk club circuit and decided to celebrate his homecoming by inviting eight musician friends to join him for the recording sessions. Singer and guitarist Moore and three of the musicians, Dónal Lunny (bouzouki and guitar), Andy Irvine (vocals, mandolin, bouzouki, hurdy-gurdy), and Liam O'Flynn (uilleann pipes, whistle) liked the sound they made on the *Prosperous* album and decided to perform together afterward. Recalling the melodies composed by seventeenth-century Turlough

O'Carolan in honor of his patrons, they named the quartet Planxty. The formation of this band opened an entirely new chapter for Irish music, and, on the back of the 1960s folk boom, sparked its full-scale revival.

On such titles as *The Well Below the Valley* (see Chapter 7, "Celtic Music on CD"), Planxty drew from a wide range of influences in experimental arrangements of traditional music. There were undertones of rock music in the layered acoustic sound, imported eastern European folk melodies, original compositions, and ancient ballads. There was passion and openness in the recordings, along with a great sense of excitement and youthful energy at the live performances. And there was the use of bouzouki as the main rhythm instrument, effortlessly uniting the uilleann pipes with the other stringed instruments. The impact was immense. Planxty effectively gave other musicians a license to experiment within the tradition, and for the first time the music was being embraced by youth culture.

Dónal Lunny left Planxty and helped form the Bothy Band, another hugely influential Irish traditional group. After their final appearance in 1979, Lunny re-joined Planxty and from the last lineup of the band, Lunny and Moore pioneered another new direction for Irish music by launching the traditional-rock fusion band Moving Hearts in 1981.

Karine Polwart (see Malinky).

The Poozies (formed 1992): Named after Ayrshire pub Poozie Nancies, a favored haunt of Robert Burns, this all-women quartet has an eclectic approach to repertoire, exploring everything from Gaelic waulking songs to lesser-known country music, pop, and original writing. Carefully worked and captivating harmonies characterize their arrangements, with high-spirited instrumental interplay crafted around the twin harps of Mary MacMaster and Patsy Seddon (the harp duo Sileas). Karen Tweed's piano accordion and Eilidh Shaw's fiddle complete the current lineup in a band that helped launch the career of Kate Rusby, who performed with them in the 1990s. The Poozies established themselves as a festival favorite from the beginning and remain a serious draw wherever they perform. *Raise Your Head* (*A Retrospective*) is a collection The Poozies sampled from three releases and features past and current members (see Chapter 7, "Celtic Music on CD").

Christine Primrose (b. 1952): This traditional singer from the Isle of Lewis has won accolades for her powerful singing since childhood and has scored victories at the National Mod, a festival of Gaelic music, and the Kilarney Pan Celtic Festival. She has traveled far from her native Isle of Lewis, introducing a wide international audience to Gaelic song with her flawless delivery and impressive repertoire. Primrose is especially admired for the emotional quality of her singing and for her pure, clear voice. She regularly collaborates with Scottish harper Alison Kinnaird. On *'S Tu Nam Chuimhne*, Primrose is joined by former and present members of Battlefield Band, jazz musicians on saxophone and trumpet, and Kinnaird on clarsach. As with her other recordings, however, the depth of emotion in her singing is most clearly found in her solo work. As reviewer Rob Adams remarked of her voice, "if there is such a phenomenon as indigenous Scottish Blues, then this is it."

Jean Redpath (b. 1937): Many Americans first discovered the pure vocal instrument of this Scotswoman in the 1980s through her earliest appearances with Garrison Keillor on public radio's live variety show *A Prairie Home Companion*. But Redpath's involvement with the United States goes back to the 1960s, when she hung out in Greenwich Village, crossing paths with Bob Dylan and other legends of the era. (Dylan has always said Scottish Border ballads and Highland folk songs were a source of inspiration for him in his songwriting, and he acknowledged this connection in accepting an honorary doctor of music degree from Scotland's St. Andrew University in 2004.) The scale of Redpath's repertoire of songs, mostly from Scotland, is astonishing. She has recorded dozens of albums, and collectively they present a valuable compendium of folk songs. The recordings on *Lowlands* offers a typically fine mix and a chance to hear the perfect marriage of Redpath's voice and Abby Newton's cello on some of the songs. These she delivers in her honest, crystal-clear mezzo-soprano, making an emotional impact every time. In the 1980s, Redpath teamed up with the late American composer and arranger Serge Hovey, with whom she collaborated in recording seven volumes of the songs of Robert Burns. A great scholar of Scottish traditional song, Redpath has also worked as a university lecturer and is much sought after to lead singing workshops and seminars.

Bonnie Rideout (b. 1962): Bonnie Rideout is the only American fiddler to have participated in the Edinburgh International Festival, in a program highlighting Scottish fiddle. She was also the first woman to hold the national fiddle title in Scotland. Her passion for the playing styles of Scotland is renowned, and she has championed the works of twentieth-century fiddlers Ron Gonnella, Arthur Scott Robertson, and Bert Murray, all dominant in their field before the current explosion of interest in Scottish fiddle worldwide. Rideout can certainly take some of the credit for the international interest in fiddle music from Scotland, especially in the United States. Her feat of winning the North American Scottish Fiddle Championship for three years running has inspired a new generation of young players to follow her path. *Celtic Circles* is a collection of tunes that transports the listener through the moods of one day's cycle, and Rideout's masterful arrangements involve Chris Caswell on harps, piper Eric Rigler (heard in the movie *Braveheart*), and Carolyn Surrick on viola da gamba.

Jeannie Robertson (1908–1975): Few traditional singers are held in such high esteem as Jeannie Robertson, and her reputation as the last century's greatest ballad interpreter continues undiminished in the twenty-first century. The late American folklorist Alan Lomax found Robertson to have "the refined mouth and the powerful throat typical of the great singer; out of it came trumpet-notes, appropriate to the big ballad, and soft flute-like tones suited to the sweet randy love songs. Jeannie was one of the angels of folksong that have kept the tradition alive and burning across all time." Robertson grew up among the community of itinerant Scottish Travelers and those origins were credited with her powerful and affecting style. Travelers had kept song and story traditions alive in their ancient oral culture and were known for astonishingly passionate singing.

Recorded in 1953, *What a Voice* was made shortly after Robertson was discovered by the late poet, songwriter, and collector Hamish Henderson. It dates from the time when Robertson was just embarking on her relationship with the international community of folklorists and so marks the earliest recording of her talking about her life with her Traveler family, along with other stories from her youth. But it is the ballads that make this album compulsory listening. They include "My Son David" (also known as "Edward"), "Andrew Lammie," and "Susan Pyatt" (or "Lord Bateman").

Kate Rusby (b. 1974): Kate Rusby's talents were marked as exceptional since the launch of her career in her early twenties, and it wasn't long before the *Daily Telegraph* had pronounced her "the brightest light in English folk music." The singer and guitarist has a unique way with a traditional song and an impressive repertoire of traditional ballads, many from Celtic origins. She brought these to the lineup of The Poozies for several years in the 1990s. Although reluctant to accept the label, she has also emerged as a major songwriter, having won the BBC Radio 2 Folk Awards prize in 2002 for "Best Original Song." This distinction came for "Who Will Sing Me Lullabies?" The United Kingdom's most listened to radio station also awarded Rusby "Folk Singer of the Year" and "Album of the Year" (for *Sleepless*) in 2000.

Rusby absorbed many of her traditional songs while growing up in her beloved native county of Yorkshire. Her parents used to sing them to her and her siblings during road trips to folk festivals. Family continues to play an important part in her musical life. Her label, Pure Records, is run with her family and her husband, John McCusker, who produces and plays on her albums. Their second production together, *Sleepless,* was short-listed for the prestigious Mercury Music Prize in 1999 and designated one of the twelve best albums of the year in any genre. The recording of *10* celebrates Rusby's first decade as a recording artist and mixes new takes of old favorites, live recordings, and previously unrecorded songs. In addition to McCusker, Rusby joins forces with accordion ace Andy Cutting, American banjo virtuoso Alison Brown, and Capercaillie's flute player Michael McGoldrick, among others. *10* serves as a great introduction to the sound of this acclaimed singer. In 2003, Rusby and McCusker collaborated to create the soundtrack for the Damien O'Donnel movie *Heartlands*.

Tommy Sands (b. 1945): This man has been singing and entertaining since before he could talk. In their small farmhouse in the Mountains of Mourne, County Down, the Sands family and their neighbors would sing away the long winter nights to the fiddle and accordion accompaniment of Tommy's parents. Tommy carried these childhood memories, along with his brothers and sister, to audiences around the world. With newly composed songs extending their repertoire of the traditional music of Ulster, the Sands family captured the attention of audiences from Carnegie Hall to Berlin's famed Fredrichstadt Palast.

Today, Sands is regarded as one of the most important songwriters in Ireland. His memorable songs have found their way into school textbooks and have been recorded in many languages. According to *The Irish Times*, this is credited to his "ability to write on serious subjects which come across as songs rather than sermons (whilst also being) extremely funny in the way he puts words together." Sands's desire to communicate has taken him to audiences beyond the concert halls and folk festivals. His weekly folk radio program, *Country Ceili*, is now regarded as a Belfast institution and is the longest-running radio program of its kind in the British Isles.

Pete Seeger, Dolores Keane, Arty McGlynn, Steve Cooney, and Ciarán Tourish and Dermot Byrne of Altan join Sands on *The Heart's a Wonder*, singing songs of the times on such thoughtful songs as "The Music of Healing" and "The Age of Uncertainty." As Pete Seeger remarks in the liner notes, "Tommy Sands and his friends are setting a good example for human beings everywhere . . . they'll use their abilities as entertainers to help pull this cantankerous human race together before we blow ourselves apart."

Susana Seivane (b. 1981): Born into a prestigious Galician musical family, Seivane was perhaps destined to follow her path into traditional music. As a dynamic and expressive gaita (Galician bagpipe) player, she has managed to remain true to the musical heritage of her family while working with contemporary instrumentation. This approach took her debut album to the finals of the U.S. Indie Awards in 2001, in the category of World and Contemporary Music. Seivane lives up to the promise of the title of *Alma de Buxo*, unlocking the "soul of the boxwood" here. An instrument maker has to wait more than a hundred years before the wood of this tree is ready to yield a set of Galician pipes. Seivane's grandfather crafted a set for her hands when she was only four years old, accounting for her early command of the instrument. By way of thanks, she invited him to join her on this exciting recording, showing the way ahead for Galician bagpipes.

Sharon Shannon (b. 1967): Button accordion virtuoso Sharon Shannon first came to the attention of many through her stint with The Waterboys, touring the world with them for eighteen months. She returned to concentrate on her solo recording work and quickly rose to become one of the brightest lights in Irish music. Shannon hails from a musical family in County Clare, an area in Western Ireland's traditional music heartland, but has expanded her repertoire to embrace musical styles from around the world, fusing the traditional and the contemporary to great effect. According to *Folk Roots* (now *fROOTS*), "she can pick a good tune at a thousand paces and her delivery and sense of arrangement is unerringly powerful."

Shannon demonstrates why she is one of the most in-demand musicians in Celtic music with the unsurpassed set of tunes on *Each Little Thing*, featuring Win Horan (Solas) and Tommy Peoples on fiddles, Steve Cooney on guitar, John McSherry on pipes and whistles, and producer Dónal Lunny playing bouzouki, bodhrán, and bass. The late Kirsty MacColl sings a transporting version of Astor Piazolla's "Libertango," on which Shannon's accordion drifts dreamily to South America.

Shooglenifty (formed 1993): Formed at a pub session in Edinburgh, this group has pioneered a folk fusion dance floor groove to mesmerizing effect. They have taken their Scottish trip-hop dance rhythms across the globe to Tokyo, the Sydney Opera House, and back again, leaving locals exhausted from dancing to the exhilarating fiddle and mandolin tunes, interwoven with bass and drum rhythms. Shooglenifty's sound is an addictive, hypnotic brand of twenty-first-century ceilidh music, as popular in the dance club as it is on the concert stage. The band is very much in demand to appear at both Celtic and world music festivals, and the excitement of their live performances is hinted at on *Venus in Tweeds* (see Chapter 7, "Celtic Music on CD").

Soig Siberil (see Kornog).

Sileas (formed 1985): In the harp duo Sileas, Patsy Seddon and Mary MacMaster have been at the forefront of the ever-expanding worldwide popularity of the small harp. Seddon and MacMaster's harp playing is rhythmic and adventurous, while their arrangements of traditional Gaelic and Scots songs, along with contemporary vocal material, are steeped in emotion. Although they came to prominence through Sileas, each is acclaimed individually and for her participation in the four-piece band The Poozies. More recently, MacMaster also joined the trio Shine, confirming her position as a seasoned and versatile performer at the leading edge of Scotland's evolving musical traditions.

Gut strung, metal strung, and Camac electro, the three harps used in *Remain in Light* have very distinct sounds. Together with Seddon's and MacMaster's creative vocal harmonies, the overall effect is at once ancient and progressive, especially when the duo drops a Bill Withers song ("Ain't No Sunshine") in among the traditional fare.

Silly Wizard (formed 1972; disbanded 1988): One of the most popular of the Scottish folk bands, Silly Wizard offered a unique combination of talents. Brothers Phil and the late Johnny Cunningham were breathtaking as a fiddle and accordion duo. Andy M. Stewart's stirring singing was riveting. The guitar and bass of Gordon Jones and Martin Hadden integrated these mighty musical forces. Add the onstage banter and nonsense, and this was a hard act to follow. All good music deserves to be heard live, and this was never more so than with Silly Wizard. The recording *Live Wizardry* captures all the favorite song and tune sets performed before a devoted U.S. audience.

Silly Wizard enjoyed great popularity at home and throughout Europe and perhaps even more so in North America, where the band toured often through the 1980s, building an avid following. Apart from Silly Wizard's reputation for unrestrained dance sets, with fiddle and accordion in full flight, the songs of Andy M. Stewart helped define the band. His rich interpretations of traditional ballads were definitive, and his own songs, such as "The Queen of Argyll" and "The Ramblin' Rover" are now folk standards and often mistaken as traditional. He has continued to build upon his reputation as a singer and song-writer in solo and duo performing since his days with Silly Wizard.

Skyedance (*see* Alasdair Fraser).

Solas (formed 1995): Multi-instrumentalist Seamus Egan formed this U.S. band whose influence is significant on both sides of the Atlantic. Egan grew up in Ireland and Philadelphia, and by age sixteen he had won all-Ireland Junior Championships on flute, whistle, tenor banjo, and uilleann pipes. In Solas, he teamed up with Irish American luminaries such as Win Horan on fiddle and accordion player John Williams, involving Ireland's John Doyle on guitar with vocalist Karan Casey through the 1990s. On *The Words That Remain*, Egan and Horan lead the instrumental sets and drive the vocals, all highly imaginatively arranged and orchestrated (see Chapter 7, "Celtic Music on CD").

Davy Spillane (b. 1959): Widely regarded as one of the world's leading uilleann pipers, Davy Spillane toured much of Europe in the 1980s with fellow members of the now-disbanded Moving Hearts. The "Hearts" lineup also included the highly influential instrumentalist and arranger Dónal Lunny and powerful singer songwriter Christy Moore. Together with Spillane, they set a new pace for the development of contemporary Irish and Celtic music.

Spillane, who also plays the low whistle, has guested on numerous albums across a diversity of recordings and has collaborated with such well-known pop and rock performers as Van Morrison, Enya, Elvis Costello, and Máire Brennan. He is in constant demand to contribute to movie soundtracks, including 1998's *Dancing at Lughnasa*.

Davy Spillane's recording career began more than three decades ago, when he was first heard on *Piper's Rock*, a combination album of young pipers. When he released his first solo album, *Atlantic Bridge*, Bela Fleck, Jerry Douglas, and a variety of American acoustic musicians joined him for the recording, which quickly became a hit in Ireland. As its title suggests, *Atlantic Bridge* meshed contemporary American and Irish sounds to create music that draws on the strengths of each component. The tracks combine American bluegrass and country rock with traditional Irish instruments and rhythmic drive. His recordings have been memorable for their breadth and the inclusion of Spillane's own compositions, which are often haunting, slow airs written for the low whistle.

Savourna Stevenson (b. 1961): Scottish harp music took on a contemporary bearing for the first time in the hands of this emphatic performer and inventive composer. Her 1984 debut *Tickled Pink* signaled Stevenson's interest in exploring the musical meeting ground of Scottish tradition and jazz, and since then, she has traveled into world music and improvisation, "her instrument thrillingly coaxed towards and across new musical frontiers" (*The Scotsman*). Her writing invariably emerges as the result of special commissions. *Calman the Dove* was recorded with uilleann piper Davy Spillane and fiddler Anne Wood, having been written to commemorate 1,400 years since the death of St. Columba on Iona. Stevenson has taken her experimental approach into her work with many well-known musicians to date, including Martin Carthy, Aly Bain, Dick Gaughan, Toumani Diabate, The Bhundu Boys, and Dónal Lunny. On *Singing the Storm*, she collaborated with the remarkable English singer June Tabor and eminent bassist Danny Thompson. The daughter of Scottish pianist and composer Ronald Stevenson, Savourna regularly composes for productions in dance, theater, television, and film.

Andy M. Stewart (see Silly Wizard).

Wendy Stewart (b. 1957): This performer, teacher, and composer of Scottish harp music established the foundation for her musical life during the 1970s, when the clarsach (Scottish harp) was benefiting from a healthy revival of interest. Stewart began playing at the age of twelve as a pupil of the respected Edinburgh teacher Jean Campbell. She went on to develop an interest in Scandanavian, Cajun, Paraguayan, and French music, contributing these flavors to the music of Ceolbeg, with whom she played for more than a decade. Stewart teaches harp courses throughout Europe and North America and has cultivated a busy solo career since her days with Ceolbeg. She carefully selected a wonderful collection of contemporary, traditional, and original material for her solo debut, *About Time,* demonstrating her gifts as both arranger and composer. With a dash of concertina and a couple of songs, the album consists mainly of Stewart on acoustic and electro harps.

Alan Stivell (b. 1944): The father of Pan-Celtic music began his career at age nine, when his father built him an ancient Celtic harp. Jord Cochevelou had devoted years to developing a prototype small harp, intending to revive the music of the long abandoned Breton instrument. When he put the harp in the hands of his son Alan Stivell Cochevelou, he would have been astonished to think he was reversing the fortunes of Breton music and fanning the flames of Celtic revival worldwide. Stivell became immersed in the music of Brittany, Wales, Scotland, Ireland, and the Isle of Man, encouraged by harp teacher Denise Megevand. He made his first recording at age eleven and broadened his instrumental base by studying at the College of Piping in Glasgow. Before long, he was applying his interest in the broad world of Celtic music to his performances, recorded arrangements, instrumental compositions, and songs, pioneering a Pan-Celticism. He took his name, Stivell, from the original Breton "Kozh Stivellou" which means "old springs," from which his family name Cochevelou was derived.

In 1974, Stivell's seminal *Renaissance of the Celtic Harp* (see Chapter 7, "Celtic Music on CD") ignited interest in Celtic harp music throughout the world and is today regarded as having realized the very goal of its title. Stivell has recorded more than twenty albums since then, embracing traditional Breton music, folk rock, orchestral epics, world music, and more recently techno and hip hop. *One Earth* features Youssou N'Dour, Khaled, Jim Kerr, and Paddy Moloney joining Stivell in this visionary album, and *Back to Breizh* has Stivell embracing the new, incorporating hip-hop beats, samples, and scratching with his trademark Celtic harp and hypnotic voice. In 2003, Stivell spent the year celebrating his half-century of harping.

Tannahill Weavers (formed 1968): Like their fellow Scots in Battlefield Band, the world has welcomed the Tannahill Weavers in tours spanning more than three decades. Countless bands have followed in their stead and been equally inspired by their musical journey. Although their arrangements are exciting and contemporary, the Tannahill Weavers have remained almost entirely acoustic in their sound. This, together with their focus on traditional material and new music in the traditional mold, contributes to the band's authenticity.

Lead singer and guitarist Roy Gullane and flute player

Phil Smillie have been at the heart of the band all along, partnering twenty assorted players who have filed through the ranks. They have also jointly created the tight harmony vocals that help define the group sound. John Martin's rhythmic fiddle playing has been a constant for many years, as has the sound of the pipes. In fact, this was the first band to feature Highland bagpipes in a Scottish folk band lineup, and they have been skirling in the Tannahill Weavers ever since. *The Best of the Tannahill Weavers* (*1979–1989*) showcases some of this classic band's earlier lineups in such favorite songs as "Auld Lang Syne" and "Johnnie Cope" and with their onetime concert opener "The Geese in the Bog/Jig of Slurs."

Simon Thoumire (b. 1970): The English concertina may seem an unlikely instrument on which to create an innovative fusion of folk and jazz. It all comes naturally to Simon Thoumire, one of the most original artists in Celtic music. On his chosen instrument, he is widely regarded as the most skilled player of his generation, having developed groundbreaking technique and repertoire. Thoumire is also an accomplished composer, with several works for concertina, small pipes, fiddle, saxophones, and clarinets, bringing together traditional and jazz elements. Thoumire and David Milligan explore the idea of improvising around traditional themes on *The Big Day In*. As the title suggests, the two recorded this collection of traditional and original music on one big day in the studio, and the album's freshness and spontaneity is their reward.

Few individuals are as enthusiastically involved in the promotion of traditional and acoustic music as Simon Thoumire. He devised the annual Young Scottish Traditional Musician of the Year Award to help boost the profile of rising talent. He is also the founder of Foot Stompin' Records, a label that aims to showcase the finest young musicians in Scottish music.

Kathryn Tickell (b. 1967): Enthusiasm for the music of the Northumbrian bagpipes has grown at quite a rate in recent years, surpassed only by enthusiasm for the music of their leading player, Kathryn Tickell. Surrounded by traditional music growing up, this exceptional musician began playing the pipes of her home region in the northeast of England (along with fiddle under legendary Shetland fiddler Tom Anderson) at the age of ten. In 1984, at the age of seventeen, she was appointed official piper to the Lord Mayor of Newcastle, the first person to hold this position for a century and a half. Since then, her playing has graced everything from recordings of traditional and progressive folk music, to the music of Sting, who also hails from Newcastle. In the hands of Tickell, the Northumbrian pipes have traveled to France, Hong Kong, Thailand, Holland, and across North America. According to *The Guardian*, "her music—a mixture of traditional tunes reinterpreted, and a growing collection of her own compositions—succeeds because she feeds off and feeds back into a tradition." On *Debateable Lands*, Tickell captures the music of the Border country and the very essence of the northeast of England in her piping and fiddling (see Chapter 7, "Celtic Music on CD").

Sheena Wellington (b. 1944): Sheena Wellington came to the attention of most Scots at the opening ceremony of the new Scottish Parliament in 1999. However, Wellington had been well known in traditional music circles for many years and was a fixture at festivals and at gatherings of the Traditional Music and Song Association (TMSA) of Scotland. Wellington was born into a family of singers and jute mill weavers in Dundee, and the city's history and musical heritage has always been an inspiration. She is well known for her repertoire of Burns songs, her interest in contemporary songwriting, and her own songs such as the modern classic, "Women o' Dundee."

Wellington assembled a grand collection of ballads, Burns songs, and new Scottish writing on *Hamely Fare*, summoning guitarist Ewan Sutherland, fiddler Pete Clark, and Neil Paterson on whistle to provide their hallmark sensitive accompaniment. For the album's most memorable piece, Wellington is unaccompanied, although millions sang along with her on television. They watched her with pride as "A Man's a Man" by Robert Burns resounded at the 1999 opening of the first Scottish Parliament in almost three hundred years. The original recording of that rendition is preserved on *Hamely Fare*.

John Whelan (b. 1959): This English-born musician is at the center of the Irish American music scene. He recorded his debut album at age fourteen and went on to win several All-Ireland titles on his chosen instrument. A truly inventive accordion player, Whelan has been involved in a variety of collaborations and musical projects, including work with fiddlers Eileen Ivers, Seamus Connolly, and Liz Knowles; guitarist Robin Bullock; and the folk rock band Kips Bay.

John Whelan crossed many a border in conceiving *Flirting With the Edge*. This music, with Latin guitarist Oscar Lopez and African kalimba player Samite Mulondo, brings Whelan's Irish button accordion out into the world. Add U.S. singers Bernadette Peters and Connie Dover, and you have an eclectic mix that still manages to remain rooted in Celtic soil.

Whistlebinkies (formed late 1960s): This long-established tradi-tional music group performs old Scottish music and new in a rich acoustic setting with lowland pipes, smallpipes, flute, clarsach, fiddle, viola, concertina, song, and drums. Indeed, the Whistlebinkies can claim the honor of being the first group to combine the three main instruments of the Scottish tradition—harp, pipes, and fiddle—in a folk group, with piper Robert Wallace being a leader in the revival of Scottish bellows-blown bagpipes. Apart from this distinction, they were also the first Scottish group to tour China in 1991 and among the first to combine traditional, classical, and art music with flute player and composer Eddie MacGuire blending this dis-ciplined approach with the more informal structure of tradi-tional music.

A Wanton Fling bears the hallmark of classic Whistle-binkies, with its mix of Scottish Gaelic and Lowland music for pipes, clarsach, fiddle, and flute, with a MacGuire compo-sition from his ballet for traditional instruments, "The Spirit of Flight." Still at the vanguard of the Scottish music scene, the Whistlebinkies offer recordings and performances of unimpeachable integrity and depth, playing only on authen-tic traditional instruments and often in a purely acoustic setting.

Wolfstone (formed 1988): This band's powerful brand of Celtic rock was born and bred in the Scottish Highlands. Electric fid-dle, electric and acoustic guitars, highland pipes, whistles, keyboards, bass, and drums combine to create one of the boldest sounds in Celtic music. Unlike many folk-rock outfits, Wolfstone actually reaches a rock audience without alienating their folk and traditional following. The band was formed by Duncan Chisholm, whose superb spirited fiddling has also been a feature of Blazin' Fiddles along the way. Guitarist and songwriter Ivan Drever made a vital contribution to the band's sound, and Stuart Eaglesham now carries lead vocals and launches the unforgettable electric guitar riffs.

If you like your Celtic music to bite you back, then you'll enjoy rocking your way through *Pick of the Litter,* the best of Wolfstone from 1991–1996. This body of work laid the foundation for the band's trademark blend of tradition and power rock, more polished in later albums but running on sheer raw energy through the first half decade. Few groups in Celtic music generate the levels of excitement seen at a Wolfstone concert. The response to the band is so enthusiastic, Denmark's international Tonder Festival invited them to appear for three consecutive years, the only band ever to be so honored.

Jennifer and Hazel Wrigley (b. 1974): Like more distant Shetland, Orkney is an archipelago lying north of the Scottish mainland. The islands' culture owes as much to a Norse heritage as it does to Celtic or Scottish influences. The Wrigley sisters' duo features fiddler Jennifer with pianist and guitarist Hazel offering truly imaginative accompaniment on piano and guitar in Orcadian-, Scottish-, and Shetland-style playing. Jennifer writes great fiddle tunes and finds no end of inspiration in the lore, landscapes, and people of the sisters' native Orkney, while Hazel's accompaniment unlocks depths in the fiddle melodies that suggest, in the case of identical twins, a splendid exaggeration of the musical compatibility famously enjoyed by siblings. In addition to the flavors of Orkney, the music of the Wrigley sisters is invigorated with jazz, blues, and rag flavors, and a touch of whimsy.

On *Mither o' the Sea,* a number of Lowland Scottish instrumentalists complement the Wrigley sisters' fiddle, guitar, and piano, but Jennifer Wrigley's use of the resonating Norwegian

Hardanger fiddle on one track serves as a reminder that we are in the far north. The sisters contribute a number of their own tunes to this collection—twelve in all—intensifying the originality of their sound.

SIX

The Music

Tens of thousands of songs, airs, dance tunes, and laments are shared across the related Celtic traditions. Some have endured through centuries; others flow into use along the way on the carrying stream of traditional music and song. Here are some leading traditional and popular titles you will recognize, along with their intriguing histories, and a selection of rising contemporary favorites you may well come to know before long.

"Ae Fond Kiss," Robert Burns: Undoubtedly one of the most beautiful and sad love songs ever written, Burns was commemorating his parting from Mrs. Agnes MacLehose (Clarinda), with whom he had enjoyed a passionate, though he claimed platonic, relationship. When she left Edinburgh to be reunited with her husband in Jamaica in December 1791, Burns committed his feelings to verse, as ever. The song has been recorded by many singers through the years and is most enhanced by simple arrangements such as Corrina Hewat offers for voice and electroharp on *My Favourite Place*.

"The Ash Grove (Llwyn Onn)," traditional: This is one of the best-known Welsh airs and was composed expressly for the harp. Free from the rigid structure of a dance tune, it takes the form of a theme and variations, very popular in the eighteenth century, when this melody first emerged. The tune was borrowed by Irish harper Turlough O'Carolan and has appeared in several other guises through the years, including in the English Morris Dance repertoire. Robin Huw Bowen has restored it to its original identity on Welsh triple harp, recording the air on *Harp Music of Wales*.

"Auld Lang Syne," Robert Burns: Each New Year, midnight shifts through the time zones and the bells of hope reverberate hourly around the world. Joining hands, crowds gather in many a land to sing one of the most popular songs in the world. That the words are not always sung accurately or fully understood does not daunt the feelings of friendship and goodwill spread internationally by the verses of "Auld Lang Syne." As he did so often and to great effect, Robert Burns shaped his verses around a fragment of an old Scots song. He sent these, along with a melody, to James Johnson, his editor for *The Scots Musical Museum*. They were published in volume five of this collection in 1796, the year Burns died. Unfortunately, "Auld Lang Syne" is popularly sung to a different tune than the one handpicked by Burns. The switch happened three years after the poet's death, when George Thomson, editor of *Scotish Airs* (*sic*), decided to set the verses to a brighter melody. When compared with Burns's own choice, it falls short in conveying the heartfelt feeling of two friends reflecting on their lasting connection, strong across time and the oceans' miles. Many Scottish singers now prefer to sing "Auld Lang Syne" to its original melody, including the Tannahill Weavers on their *Best of... 1979–1989* album and Jean Redpath from her collaboration with the late American arranger Serge Hovey for *The Songs of Robert Burns, Volume One*. Once sung or heard the way Burns intended, it is difficult to revert to the popular tune.

"Bonnie Banks o' Loch Lomond," traditional: Most people approach these verses as a simple celebration of the landscape to which the song has brought worldwide fame. And most singers have given it a jaunty interpretation, including the American jazz vocalist Maxine Sullivan, who had a hit with "Loch Lomond" in the 1950s. But wouldn't verses imagined to be the last words of a condemned man be more effectively sung as a lament? The song was written at the time of the Jacobite Rising of 1745. The Jacobite army was in retreat from Derby following its invasion of England. As they approached the Scottish border, several of the walking wounded could struggle no farther and fell back from the rest of the troop in Carlisle, just south of Scotland. Many were picked up by English soldiers and thrown into Carlisle jail. Written during this period, the song tells of two Scottish prisoners held together in the jail and hinges around the old Celtic belief that if you die away from your homeland, you return by an underground spirit route called The Low Road. One soldier was to be set free and the other executed for his part in the Jacobite Rising against the Hanovarian king. The two prisoners' release and execution were timed for the same hour. The freed man would travel home to Scotland the conventional way, tramping wearily for many miles by The High Road. The condemned man, traveling with the speed of a spirit by The Low Road, would be transported instantly at the moment of death, arriving home first, but never seeing his true love again. Almost all versions of this song are sung with a cheeriness that misrepresents its origins. However, Runrig takes it at a slower pace and transforms it into an anthem with their only too willing live audience on *Once in a Lifetime*.

"Bonny Barbara Allen," traditional: The source of this simple ballad of romantic tragedy is unknown, but written introductions in ballad collections often open with the quotation from the seventeenth-century English diarist Samuel Pepys, "In perfect pleasure I was to hear her [Mrs. Knipp, the actress] sing her little Scotch song of Barbary Allen." The song's earliest written versions are certainly in Scots, but the ballad seems to have been common throughout the British Isles and Ireland. It found its way into American songbooks early, after which it changed very little and went on to enjoy the widest geographical spread of any ballad in the United States. Reclaiming her musical roots and early influences, Dolly Parton recorded a moving version of Barbara Allen on her album *Heartsongs*.

"Both Sides the Tweed," Dick Gaughan: Gaughan created this song from a poem by James Hogg, the eighteenth-century Border writer and shepherd (Hogg's Jacobite Relics). His was a critique on the Act of Union between Scotland and England, a move that was almost wholly unsupported by the general Scottish public at the time of signing in 1707. Because Scotland didn't have a democratically elected parliament in those days, few in power paid any heed to anything but the forces of political and economic self-interest. Dick's re-working gave the Hogg verses a more contemporary bearing and developed his theme of friendship crossing from each bank of the River Tweed. (The Tweed is the natural boundary along some eastern stretches of the Scottish border with England.) Apart from Gaughan's own riveting version on *Handful of Earth*, Capercaillie's sensitive arrangement on *Sidewaulk* is another classic.

"Caledonia," Dougie MacLean: One of Scotland's best-known songwriters, MacLean penned these homesick verses in the 1970s when he was an itinerant musician, busking with his fiddle in France. He has certainly written many more substantial songs since, but the innocent sincerity of this early offering has captured hearts well beyond Scottish shores. Rock singer Frankie Miller had a commercial hit with the song in the early 1990s, and it has also been recorded by an international assortment of artists and sung as an anthem at many a gathering. As his stature as a musician grew, MacLean spent some years avoiding performing "Caledonia" but has warmed to the song again in recent times, recording it live in 2000 at the Port Fairy Folk Festival in Australia for his album *Live from the Ends of the Earth.*

"Christ Child's Lullaby (Taladh Chriosda)," traditional: Father Allan Macdonald of Eriskay in the Outer Hebrides first collected and published this traditional Scots Gaelic hymn in the nineteenth century. There are several different English translations, one even having been arranged by the late composer of American Popular Song Alec Wilder and recorded by folk singer Shawn Colvin on *Holiday Songs and Lullabies*. The translation by Gaelic singer Kenna Campbell retains the true simplicity of the original Gaelic verses, well conveyed by Sheena Wellington on *Clearsong*.

"Danny Boy," traditional/lyric Fred Weatherly: Some songs are simply sung too much, and we forget why they became popular in the first place. For that reason, it would be easy to overlook "Danny Boy" for inclusion on this list. However, the key to this song's long-lived appeal has to be its melody. Jane Ross of Limavady published it with no title in 1855, having heard the tune played locally. Since then, it has been known as the "Derry Air." Different lyrics have been attached to the melody through the years, but the popular ones were written by Fred Weatherly, an English barrister and opera librettist. As a song, its notoriety grew with the Irish tenors of the vaudeville stage. It still stands as one of the most sentimental songs ever written and is always most beloved among the Irish diaspora. Rediscover its essential appeal through the melody alone with guitarist El McMeen on *Irish Guitar Encores,* or hear Sinéad O'Connor uncover the song's unexpected power on Davy Spillane's album *The Sea of Dreams.*

"Eliz Iza," traditional: This traditional folk song from the mountains of Brittany captures the ethereal beauty of Breton melody. Alan Stivell shared it with the world on his seminal *Renaissance of the Celtic Harp,* and it has since come to symbolize the realised promise in the title of Stivell's album.

"Farewell to Erin," traditional: Few tunes better typify the energy and passion of Irish fiddle playing. It was performed by Kevin Burke with The Bothy Band for *After Hours,* their legendary live recording in Paris in 1978, and has since been picked up by hordes of musicians on both sides of the Atlantic.

"Miss McLeod's Reel," traditional: This tune represents hundreds that have traveled thousands of miles—popular at the Celtic source and given new life in the New World. On

the fiddles, bows, and banjos of the Appalachian moun-
taineers, a Scottish dance tune like "Miss McLeod's Reel" became the old-time standard "Hop High Ladies" or "Did You
Ever See the Devil Uncle Joe?" "Lord MacDonald's Reel" became "Leather Breeches," and tunes from as far afield as
Shetland became Southern music standards like "Soldiers
Joy." Dance tunes such as these from Scotland and Ireland became a foundation in the repertoires of old-time, bluegrass,
and country music. Irish band Craobh Rua includes Miss
MacLeod's in a set of reels as part of their involvement in the
live recording of *The Shetland Sessions, Volume One.* To hear
what happens to the tune when it crosses the ocean, listen to
Boys of the Lough's version, "Hop-High Ladies" from *Good
Friends, Good Music.*

"Molly Malone," traditional: Children around the world
sing this Dublin street song as "Cockles and Mussels." In
keeping with many songs for children, it is actually a tragic
story. Set in old Dublin, a street vendor dies in poverty of a
fever, leaving her ghost to call her street cry and wheel her
barrow through the streets. The creepy outcome possibly ex-
plains the appeal of the song to children, who usually offset
its true mood by singing it in a cheerful, upbeat manner. Bohinta captures the eerie sadness of the song in an inspired
arrangement on *Bohinta.*

"Music for a Found Harmonium," Simon Jeffes: Certainly
not traditional, and hardly Celtic, this contemporary tune has
been picked up by several bands since it first appeared on the
Penguin Café Orchestra album *Broadcasting from Home* in
1984. When Patrick Street recorded the tune for *Irish Times*
in 1990, it found its Celtic audience. As the story goes, Simon
Jeffes was staying in Kyoto after the Penguin Café Orchestra's

first tour to Japan in 1982. Out strolling one evening, he saw a harmonium sitting on a pile of garbage in a back alley. The instrument was in good condition and perfect working order, so he checked that it really was being discarded before rescuing it and composing this mesmerizing tune on it some time later.

"My Lagan Love," traditional: Many a traditional Irish love song is more than it seems. "My Lagan Love" has all the credentials of an *amhrain*, the love songs that populated Irish music from the late seventeenth century. But it sounds a tone of defiant political undercurrent. It appeared at a time when it was forbidden by law to write openly about Ireland. So poets and songsmiths took to likening Ireland to a beautiful woman, and expressed their desire for freedom and their love of the land through a poetic sexual desire. Sinéad O'Connor has the voice and emotional delivery required for unearthing all the layers of this song in *Sean-Nós Nua*.

"Niel Gow's Lament for the Death of His Second Wife," **Niel Gow:** This is often cited as the most beautiful fiddle tune ever written. It is certainly the best-known composition of Perthshire fiddler Gow, who left a legacy of tunes that continue to inspire Scottish musicians. He dedicated this melody to his second wife of thirty years, Margaret Urquhart, who died in 1805. Many artists have recorded this lament. Pete Clark and Dougie Maclean both live within a few short miles of Gow's cottage in Inver, Perthshire. Clark's version on *Even Now* and MacLean's on *Tribute* both capture the elegance and emotion of this great tune.

"Paddy's Green Shamrock Shore," traditional: Almost thirty percent of the population of Ireland emigrated in the years following the Great Famine, most to North America. Dozens of ballads describe their desperate crossing and the destitution that greeted many of them upon arrival in New York, Quebec, Boston, and Baltimore. This song is particularly descriptive of the crossing from Derry Quay, toward hopes of a new life upon arrival in New York. It is especially associated with Dolores Keane, who used it to launch her outstanding collaboration with John Faulkner and Eamonn Curran, *Farewell to Eirinn.*

"Si Bheag Si Mhor," Turlough O'Carolan: Carolan is remembered as the last of the itinerant Irish bards. After smallpox robbed him of his sight, he was schooled on the harp and took to the road at age twenty-one as a novice harper. His first patron, Squire George Reynolds, was not impressed by Carolan's debut performance and suggested that he try his hand at composing. Reynolds then told him of a battle that had taken place nearby among the "good people," two rival fairy clans who inhabited adjacent hills, and he left him to write a song about the conflict. "Si Bheag Si Mhor" ("The Little Fairy Hill and the Big Fairy Hill") pleased Squire Reynolds and set Carolan on the road to composing well over two hundred tunes, many in honor of his patrons (planxtys). Although the words are still known, it is the melody of "Si Bheag Si Mhor" that lives on as Carolan's most popular composition. By 2001, Carolan biographer Art Edelstein had documented one hundred twelve recordings of this tune, including his own from his *Fair Melodies* book and CD. Pierre Bensusan's guitar arrangement on *Musiques* and the classic versions by Planxty from *Planxty* and by late Chieftains harper Derek Bell on *Carolan's Receipt* highlight the tune's beauty as well as any.

"Song for Ireland," Phil Colclough: This wish for peace throughout Ireland has become one of the most frequently performed contemporary Irish songs both in Ireland and farther afield. Mary Black took it to an international audience when she recorded it with De Dannan in the early 1980s. She subsequently included it on her album *Collected*, and Dick Gaughan's rendition on *Handful of Earth* is considered a classic.

"The Parting Glass," traditional: These bittersweet verses comprise one of the best-known farewell songs in Ireland and Scotland. Before "Auld Lang Syne" took hold, it was the most popular parting song sung in Scotland and a traditional anthem for the close of gatherings large and small. Irish trio The Voice Squad captures the communal quality of "The Parting Glass" with an unaccompanied setting in three-part harmony on *Many's the Foolish Youth*.

"Wild Mountain Thyme," traditional: This song would be the one guaranteed to get any pub crowd singing, wherever you happened to be in Scotland or Ireland. Its infectious chorus and hopeful romantic note sets the crowd swaying back and forth even if the chorus is all they know. For sheer, unbridled sing-along fun, you can't beat the version by The Corries on *The Silver Collection, 1966–1991*.

"Ye Banks and Braes o' Bonnie Doon," Robert Burns: The Bard's verses could easily dominate any list of the best Celtic songs, and rightly so. This song of lost love has everything we expect from Burns: a beautiful melody, a pastoral setting, and a good, sharp tug at the heartstrings. Dougie MacLean's version is one to listen for on *Tribute*.

SEVEN

Celtic Music on CD

Every CD collection needs some Celtic music, but where do you begin? There is almost too much to choose from, with more new releases coming out each day. Sort through the suggestions in this chapter, according to your preference for vocals, instrumentals, ensembles, solo artists or various artist compilations, and at least you'll be on your way. Try not to limit yourself to sampling only the CDs listed here: There's so much more to be discovered!

A' Jock Tamson's Bairns, **Jock Tamson's Bairns (Greentrax):** For this album, two early recordings by a seminal Scottish band resurface from more than two decades ago. The first, *Jock Tamson's Bairns,* had become available only on cassette, and the second, *The Lasses Fashion* had been long since unavailable on any format. And yet they each offered wonderful acoustic treatment of traditional Scottish dance tunes and songs that still have a contemporary freshness about them. So this re-release is more than welcome. English guitiarist, singer, and songwriter Richard Thompson picked *The Lasses Fashion* as one of his top ten all-time favorites in the influential *Q Magazine*, ranking it alongside recordings by Elvis, The Byrds, and other nonfolk artists.

With both Rod Paterson and the late Tony Cuffe contributing vocals and Jack Evans leading the rhythmic charge, these albums are both lively and affecting. Rod Paterson leads "Lady Keith's Lament" and Tony Cuffe "The Hieland Soldier" for two standout songs, with "The Lasses Fashion" opening medley setting the rhythmic standard (vocal and instrumental).

Ballroom, **De Dannan (WEA):** De Dannan/De Danann (a name so often misspelled the spelling became something of a game with the band through the years) is hailed for many significant contributions, including the number of outstanding Irish female vocalists introduced by the band. Dolores Keane was the first and remained with the group for some years before developing her solo career. Also with De Dannan toward the end of that time was cellist Caroline Lavelle, whose instrument and vocal harmonies provided the perfect substructure for Keane's remarkable voice. The immigration/love song "Teddy O'Neill" and Eric Bogle's anti-war ballad "All the Fine Young Men" are perfect examples of their work together. Meanwhile, with Frankie Gavin on fiddle and the singular lineup of Máirtín O'Connor on accordion, Alec Finn on bouzouki, and Johnny McDonagh on Irish percussion, the tune sets—"John Kimmel's" and "Eleanor Neary's"—are as engaging as can be (instrumental and vocal).

Best of Battlefield Band/Temple Records: A 25-Year Legacy, **Battlefield Band/various artists (Temple Records):** In two and a half decades of touring and recording, this

Scots group has logged more than twenty albums to date, not to mention an incredible number of air miles. Selecting one album to represent the contributions of several lineups is just not possible. As founding member and current leader Alan Reid says, "I've been in a succession of great bands, and they're all called Battlefield Band." Better to follow their sound through the decades by tasting nineteen tracks from nineteen albums, selected by their long-time manager and producer Robin Morton. The collection includes great arrangements of fiddle and pipe tune sets and such classic songs as Robert Burns's autobiographical verses "Rantin' Rovin' Robin," sung by Sylvia Barnes, one of three women singers to have performed with the band. Also included is Brian McNeill's remarkable song "The Yew Tree" and the late Davy Steele's anthem "The Last Trip Home." The second CD in this set marks the first twenty-five years of Temple Records, founded by original member of Boys of the Lough, producer Robin Morton. Through Temple Records, Morton introduced us to harper Alison Kinnaird, Gaelic singer Christine Primrose, and multi-instrumentalist John McCusker. All are included in the twenty-five-track collection, along with other luminaries from the world of Scottish traditional music (instrumental and vocal).

The Best of The Bothy Band, **The Bothy Band (Green Linnet):** This was the first band to bring the drive of rock 'n' roll to traditional music, although the mostly acoustic lineup was always fiercely respectful to the traditional roots of their instrumental and vocal music. They first recorded in 1975, and excitement spread throughout traditional music enthusiasts in Ireland and Britain. By 1979, the group members had gone their separate ways and the name of The Bothy Band consigned to the legendary status it has held ever since.

The Best of... collection samples from the band's four albums. It re-introduces such favorite songs as the multi-harmony "Fionnghuala" and "Do You Love an Apple?" sung by vocalist and keyboard player Tríona Ní Dhomhnaill. For most of the band's history, instrumental sets brought together the remarkable lineup of Kevin Burke's fiddle, Matt Molloy's flute, Paddy Keenan's pipes, and the rhythm of string players Dónal Lunny and Mícheál Ó Domhnaill. The reel set "The Green Groves of Erin and the Flowers of Red Hill," taken from a live album recorded in Paris, is but one stellar example (instrumental and vocal).

***The Blue Idol,* Altan (Narada):** Any Altan album would be worthy of special recommendation. This one has all the hallmarks of the band's unrivalled sound: Mairéad Ní Mhaonaigh's shimmering voice, warmer with every recording, the paired fiddles of Ní Mhaonaigh and Ciaran Tourish, Dermot Byrne's expressive button accordion, and the praiseworthy list goes on. Giving this album an added dimension is the guest roster, including Paul Brady, Dónal Lunny, Dolly Parton, Liam O'Flynn, Anna Ní Mhaonaigh, Steve Cooney, and others. These artists augment Altan's core sound sympathetically on many tracks, including the love song "The Pretty Young Girl" and the ancient ditty "Uncle Rat." The "Gweebarra Bridge" set eases seamlessly from a slip jig into a reel and is a great example of the lift and lilt that have made Altan's sound so irresistible (vocal and instrumental).

***The Brendan Voyage,* Shaun Davey (Tara):** Almost one thousand years before Columbus sailed to North America, an ancient manuscript chronicled the voyage of an Irish monk who was thought to have navigated the Atlantic Ocean and reached the shores of Newfoundland. The possibility that

St. Brendan the Navigator actually discovered America in the sixth century was given credence by explorer Tim Serverin's successful reconstruction of the voyage in 1977. The seafaring adventures of the sixth-century monk and the twentieth-century explorer inspired Irish composer Shaun Davey, whose musical narrative *The Brendan Voyage* chronicled the adventures and was the first to combine Irish traditional and classical instrumentation. Central to the work is the uilleann piping of Liam O'Flynn, whose pipes dart among the billows of the orchestra and create real excitement as they rise above the waves of music (instrumental).

Canan Nan Gaidheal, **Catherine-Ann MacPhee (Greentrax):** This album marked the recording debut of a highly respected Gaelic singer from the Island of Barra in the Outer Hebrides. MacPhee's remarkable voice is backed by some of the great names in Scottish music, including William (Billy) Jackson, Tony Cuffe, Iain MacDonald, and John Martin, all members of groundbreaking band Ossian at one time or another. Producer Jim Sutherland is a multi-instrumentalist and percussionist, and he successfully harnessed the directness and power of MacPhee's voice. The album's title track is a rallying song by the twentieth-century poet Murdo Mac-Farlane. His words address the present state and future of the Gaelic language. Billy Jackson arranged the track, which builds from the strings of his clarsach toward the anthemic Highland pipes of Iain MacDonald (vocal).

Capernaum, **Tannahill Weavers (Green Linnet):** This classic Scottish band has sustained a remarkably consistent sound and lineup through the years, albeit with a few of the inevitable comings and goings. This album is, therefore, both recent and vintage Tannies, with the group's fundamental blend of pipes, flute, guitar, fiddle, bouzouki, bodhrán, and voices hitting the mark, as ever. They celebrate Scotland's living musical traditions by blending new pipe tunes such as "The Unicorn" and "Trip to Pakistan" with band compositions including Phil Smillie's "Sound of Taransay," traditional fare, and one of their rare performances of the songs of their namesake Robert Tannahill, "The Braes o' Balquidder" (vocal and instrumental).

Choice Language, **Capercaillie (Vertical):** This pioneering band has seared through musical boundaries with almost every release in the past two decades. Their sophisticated, commercial blend of ancient and contemporary instrumentals and vocals have both elevated the profile of Gaelic song and given it a new appeal to Gaelic speakers and non-Gaels alike, especially through the unique vocal talents of Karen Matheson. Recent albums have been particularly genre leaping, taking Gaelic song toward a world music fusion. In *Choice Language,* Donald Shaw's synthesisers, sampling, and programming sit comfortably among the more acoustic instrumental fabric of Michael McGoldrick's whistle, flute, and pipes; Charlie McKerron's fiddle; and the bouzouki and guitar of Manus Lunny. As is often the case, progressive arrangements of ancient Gaelic *puirt-a-beul* (mouth music) and waulking songs are a hallmark of Capercaillie's sound, and a blend of "Air Fair an La/Cailleach Liath Rathasai" continues that splendid custom (vocal and instrumental).

Crossing the Bridge, **Eileen Ivers (Sony):** As the daughter of Irish immigrants, Eileen Ivers grew up in the culturally diverse neighborhood of the Bronx, New York. So although she is an accomplished player of Irish traditional music, the multicultural sounds of her childhood are fully expressed in her fiddling, and Ivers is a world musician in the fullest sense. On this album, she experiments with ideas and influences from flamenco, Cuba, jazz, bluegrass, and hip hop, blending them all with Irish musical roots in her unique, pioneering way. From the cheeky experimentation of "Crossing the Bridge" to the breathtaking beauty of "Dear Irish Boy," this adventurous album pushes the notion of traditional music into new territory (instrumental).

Debateable Lands, **Kathryn Tickell (Park):** Through her recording, tours, and broadcasts, Kathryn Tickell has taken the music of the sweet-sounding Northumbrian pipes to international audiences. Although she has added the sound of her instrument to Sting's dreamy "Fields of Barley" and other recordings, it is to the music of England's Border country that she always returns, capturing the very essence of the northeast of England in her piping and fiddling. On the title suite of this album she gets to the heart of the history of the Borderlands between England and Scotland, the Debateable Lands, at one time a haven for outlaws, cattle reivers (raiders), and feud makers (instrumental).

Essential, **The Easy Club (Eclectic):** The members of this influential band built their sound upon the rhythms of Scottish pipe music and the energy of jazz and early acoustic rock 'n' roll. Inspired by Duke Ellington's comment that only jazz and Scottish music swing, they conceived the notion of "Scottish Rhythm and Swing" that permeated their songs and tune sets. Rod Paterson's voice, one of the best suited of any "folk" singer to the jazz idiom, is complemented by vigorous rhythm from Jim Sutherland and Jack Evans, John Martin's fiddle, and early contributions from concertina player Norman Chalmers. With this combination, The Easy Club helped bridge the gap between the jazz and traditional music worlds, creating a climate of rhythmic and harmonic experimentation in Scotland and beyond. This album includes some previously unreleased tracks and represents all three releases by the band with such classic songs as "The Diamond" and "Black Is the Colour" and tune sets including "The Easy Club Reel and Janine's Reel" ably demonstrating their unique musical approach (instrumental and vocal).

Fused, **Michael McGoldrick (Compass):** Flute and whistle player and uilleann piper McGoldrick surrounds himself with a dazzling assortment of musicians from the British Isles and Ireland for this exciting album. Included are his Capercaillie compatriots, including keyboard specialist Donald Shaw, who produced the album. McGoldrick's own composition, "Waterman's," sets the progressive tone of the album, and "Fisher Street" brings together traditional instrumentation and brass, a rare combination pioneered by Moving Hearts and Quebec band La Bottine Souriante that almost always works very well (instrumental).

Handful of Earth, **Dick Gaughan (Green Linnet):** His career has given us many highlights, but this may yet be Gaughan's definitive album. First issued in 1981, it is frequently cited as one of the most important recordings of the 1980s. Gaughan's fiery passion and breathtaking guitar technique are on full display on his mesmerizing delivery of the Burns song "Now Westlin Winds," Phil Colclough's "Song for Ireland," and Gaughan's own "Both Sides the Tweed" (vocal).

Her Infinite Variety: Celtic Women in Music and Song, **various artists (Green Linnet):** This two-CD set features some of the most outstanding singers and musicians from Ireland, Scotland, and the United States and draws on more than two decades' worth of recorded material. Vocal tradition bearers and instrumental innovators are equally represented, and the collection offers many a highlight, including Mairéad Ni Mhaonaigh and Altan with "The Flower of Magherally," Niamh Parsons and The Loose Connections with "Clohinne Winds," and fiery instrumental sets from Liz Carroll and Sharon Shannon (vocal and instrumental).

***Idir an Dá Sholas (Between the Two Lights),* Maighread and Tríona Ní Dhomhnaill with Dónal Lunny (Green Linnet):** Tapping into their intuitive sisterly musical connection, these highly influential singers present a sparkling collection of songs, many of which were handed down within their family. They first performed and recorded together in the 1970s in the quartet Skara Brae along with brother Micheál, with whom Tríona went on to form the legendary groups the Bothy Band and Nightnoise. Singing together again in unison and harmony, this collection is mostly in Irish. Highlights include "Liostáil mé le Sáirsint," "Méilte Cheann Dubhrann," and the children's song "Tidy Ann," on which they are joined by a number of friends with *Riverdance*'s Bill Whelan, credited with having played the kitchen sink (vocal).

***Inchcolm,* William Jackson (Linn):** On this album, composer and multi-instrumentalist William (Billy) Jackson developed his interest in the moods of early Scottish music, his collaborations with orchestral strings, and his own composing skills, having written almost all the music for the album. From simple arrangements for clarsach (Scottish harp), flute, and cello, to dramatic epic works for pipes, whistle, percussion, clarsach, and orchestral strings, the music ebbs and flows through contemporary Celtic and medieval moods. Included is the momentous "Corryvreckan," and "Salve Splendor," a haunting chant from the thirteenth-century Inchcolm Antiphoner, featuring the singing of Mae McKenna (instrumental and vocal).

Andy Irvine Paul Brady, **Andy Irvine and Paul Brady (Mulligan):** With the breakup of the first Planxty lineup in 1975, two members decided to combine talents on a recording. Like so many milestone albums in Irish music, fellow Planxty alumnus Dónal Lunny served as producer. Bouzouki, mandolin, and cittern are now commonly heard in Celtic music, but they made for a highly unusual combination at the time, especially when combined with hurdy-gurdy and harmonium. Not surprisingly, this exotic mix immediately caught the attention of fellow musicians, reviewers, and the folk music community, for whom this album has remained a classic. Paul Brady's solo performance on the ballad "Arthur McBride" and the Irvine/Brady collaboration on "Mary and the Soldier," on which Kevin Burke and Dónal Lunny guest, are timeless tracks (vocal and instrumental).

Lead the Knave, **Arty McGlynn and Nollaig Casey (Starc):** With partners guitarist Arty McGlynn and fiddler Nollaig Casey each moving further into traditional music, it was only a matter of time before they started playing together. Their musical paths crossed again and again and eventually, in 1984, they married. 1990's *Lead the Knave* was McGlynn and Casey's first recording together, followed by the excellent *Causeway* in 1995. Each is considered a masterpiece of Irish music. Dónal Lunny joins the pair as producer, and the combination is unbeatable throughout. From the opening title tune (a McGlynn original) to one of the most moving recorded renditions of "Caoineadh Eoghain Ruadh" ("Lament for Owen Roe O'Neill") played by Casey on fiddle and viola, and on to such traditional fare as "The Cottage in the Grove" reel set, this album shines throughout (instrumental).

Lost in the Loop, **Liz Carroll (Green Linnet):** After a ten-year break from recording, Liz Carroll released this remarkable collection of twenty-five tunes, half of which she composed. The descriptive title reel is a reference to the stressful business of driving through the congested streets of her home city. It's a reminder to us of how much her music is steeped in the Irish American communities of Chicago, a thriving center of Irish traditional music since the nineteenth century. With both parents born in Ireland, Carroll's own roots have been cultivated in the United States. Her air, "Lament of the First Generation," speaks to the cultural confusion that can arise when your heart is pulled toward two different lands. With this, and the opening set of reels "Sevens, Michael Kennedy's and The Cup of Tea," this is obviously the sound of a musician at the very peak of her powers (instrumental).

Máire, **Máire Brennan (Atlantic):** All but one of the songs on this remarkable album were written or co-written by Brennan, known internationally as the voice of the Irish family-based band Clannad. This album is also something of a family affair, involving three of Brennan's sisters on backup vocals, which accounts for the intimacy of the luxuriant, harmonic textures. This was her first departure from the Clannad lineup, and Dónal Lunny's strings, keyboards, percussion, and co-production helped create an individual inflection for Brennan, especially on the arresting "Against the

Wind" and "Voices of the Land" and on the gentler "Cé Leis" and "Oró" (vocal).

The Music and Song of Greentrax: The Best of Scottish Music, various artists (Greentrax): This two-CD set of the independent label's leading artists is anyone's ideal introduction to Scottish music. The label has helped many musicians reach wider audiences and has debuted a number of well-established artists, such as Catherine-Anne MacPhee and Shooglenifty. Both are included on this collection, along with Ceolbeg, Mairi MacInnes, Gordon Duncan, Whistlebinkies, Jean Redpath, Seelyhoo, and many more (instrumental and vocal).

Natalie MacMaster Live, Natalie Macmaster (Greentrax): Hear one of the most inspired and driven of fiddlers as she should be heard: live. This two-CD set captures all the energy and excitement of MacMaster, her six-piece band, and team of seven step dancers performing onstage at The Living Arts Center, Mississauga, Ontario, twenty years after her stage debut. The euphoric concert hall audience on disc one is contrasted with disc two's intimacy and revelry at a square dance in Glencoe Mills, Cape Breton. Here guitarist Dave MacIsaac joins MacMaster, along pianist Joel Chiasson, and a room full of dancers in all their foot-stomping glory. It is Cape Breton fiddling heard at the heart of the community that nurtured Natalie MacMaster and her legendary Uncle Buddy. "The Fairy Dance" set from the concert recording and "Grand Promenade" from the square dance are highlights (instrumental).

Pipedreams, Davy Spillane (Tara): This spellbinding Irish performer is one of the most widely heard musicians in all of

Celtic music. His collaborations cross into every genre and have led to Spillane contributing to theme music for many soundtracks. This album spotlights his skills as a composer and as a virtuoso on uilleann pipes and whistle. From the fervent "Undertow" and "Morning Wings" to the passionate "Midnight Walker," Spillane and his band have created an exhilarating soundtrack worthy of any trip on the open road, speakers at full volume, skylight open, wind in the hair (instrumental).

Première: Music from Brittany Kornog, **various artists (Green Linnet):** With irresistible Breton dances, Scottish songs, instrumental solos, and onstage banter, Kornog first took their music to the United States in 1983, causing excitement wherever they appeared. The atmosphere was captured on this live album, recorded at the Coffeehouse Extempore in Minneapolis. It features three virtuosos of traditional Breton music: Soïg Siberil on guitar, Jean-Michel Veillon on flute and bombarde, and Christian Lemaitre on fiddle. Their sound is intermingled with the bouzouki and mandolin of Jamie McMenemy, who brings ballads from his native Scotland into the mix, setting them among the rhythms and melodies of Brittany (instrumental and vocal).

Primary Colours, **Chantan (Culburnie):** This album of songs is arranged around three finely tuned and beautifully harmonized voices, belonging to Christine Kydd, Elspeth Cowie, and Corrina Hewat. The material is mostly from the Scots tradition, but influences drift in, to wonderful effect, from jazz and blues. Guitar and harp add textures to imaginative and highly appealing arrangements of such gems as "Slave's Lament," "The Collier Laddie," and "Boser Girls" (vocal).

Raise Your Head (A Retrospective), **The Poozies (Compass):** This collection samples from three releases by one of the United Kingdom's leading traditional groups and features past and current members, Patsy Seddon, Mary MacMaster, Karen Tweed, Sally Barker, and Kate Rusby. The unique sound of The Poozies relies upon Seddon and MacMaster's harp duo (Sileas), upon which The Poozies layer accordion, fiddle, guitar, and stunning vocals. The music draws from the traditional well, and from anywhere else that takes the fancy of band members, and may include lush harmonies on a Sally Barker original such as "We Built Fires," or jaunty, harp-led traditional melodies such as "Willie's Old Trousers" (vocal and instrumental).

Renaissance of the Celtic Harp, **Alan Stivell (Rounder):** This album undoubtedly introduced many to the timeless beauty of the Celtic harp, and to Breton, Scots, Irish, and Welsh melodies inaccessible via mainstream music channels at the time of its release in 1975. Stivell sparked the revival of the small harp not only in his native Brittany, but throughout the Celtic world and beyond, and was first to explore fully the appeal of Pan-Celtic tune combinations. His "Gaeltacht" medley fills side two of the original vinyl release and is a spellbinding musical journey through the Scottish Hebrides, Ireland, and the Isle of Man. The current interest in Celtic harps, from traditional to New Age music, is traceable to the impact of this album. It would appear on anyone's list as one of the classic recordings of Celtic music (instrumental).

A River of Sound: The Changing Course of Irish Traditional Music, **various artists (Hummingbird):** Ever eager to explore the traditional roots and contemporary branches of Irish music, pianist and composer Mícheál Ó Súilleabháin devised a television series for BBC Northern Ireland and Rá-dio Telefis Éireann. One hundred and thirty musicians con-tributed to the series, and a good number appear in these musical highlights from the television programs. They in-clude fiddling from Eileen Ivers, Nollaig Casey, Altan's Cia-ran Tourish, and De Dannan's Frankie Gavin; singing from Christy Moore; and button accordion from Máirtín O'Connor and Altan's Dermot Byrne. Ó Súilleabháin's piano joins the Irish Chamber Orchestra for his own "Ah Sweet Dancer," with Eileen Ivers soloing. The album's musical pinnacle, "A River of Sound," brings together players from diverse back-grounds, including internationally renowned Scottish percus-sionist Evelyn Glennie. This ambitious project helps to define the position of Irish traditional music in the third millen-nium as it taps into the past and reaches toward the wider world (instrumental and vocal).

***Scotland the Real: Music from Contemporary Caledonia,* various artists (Smithsonian Folkways):** This collection was released to coincide with "Scotland at the Smithsonian," a showcase of Scottish traditional and contemporary arts fea-tured at the 2003 Smithsonian Folklife Festival. Twenty of to-day's finest instrumentalists, singers, and songwriters are included, giving insight into the centuries-old journey of Scottish music and a feeling for where it is all heading in the hands of this vibrant generation. Instrumental power from the Tannahill Weavers, Brian McNeill, and Fiddler's Bid complement more than a dozen timeless, mostly contempo-rary songs. They include Cilla Fisher's version of "Norland Wind," Malinky's "Thaney," and Jim Malcolm's "Jimmy's Gone to Flanders." The collection was compiled by this au-thor and Smithsonian Curator Nancy Groce (instrumental and vocal).

Seal Song, **Ossian (Iona/Lismor):** In lineups spanning more than three decades, Ossian has featured many of the leading names in Scottish music. William Jackson's Scottish harp, whistles, and uilleann pipes were always at the nucleus of most arrangements, as were the voices of Billy Ross and the late Tony Cuffe at different times in the band's history. This album combines the talents of William Jackson and fiddler John Martin, with Tony Cuffe and Jackson's sadly missed brother George. The hypnotic "Fisherman's Song for Attracting Seals" and Tony Cuffe's brilliant setting of "The Road to Drumleman" help set the tone of a dreamy and transporting collection (vocal and instrumental).

The Seville Suite, **Bill Whelan (Celtic Heartbeat):** Just a couple of years before his phenomenal success with *Riverdance,* composer and producer Bill Whelan was invited to commemorate Ireland's involvement in Expo '92 at Seville with a musical commission. He proposed to turn his attention to telling the story of Red Hugh O'Donnell and his army's flight to Spain after their defeat at the Battle of Kinsale (1601). Prince Philip of Spain protected them as they fled to Galicia, from which landscape Whelan derives much of his inspiration for *The Seville Suite.* Uilleann piper Davy Spillane, accordion player Máirtín O'Connor, and members of the Galician band Milliadoiro join the RTE Concert Orchestra for this epic work. "The Road to La Coruña" is an album highlight, as is the inclusion of the "Timedance" collaboration with Dónal Lunny for an earlier performance by Planxty in 1981 (instrumental).

Sink Ye-Swim Ye, **Finn MacCuill (R2):** First released in 1978, this album represents the only recorded memory of a once very promising lineup. Fortunately, after years of being out of print, it is available once again. The recording is note-worthy for its imaginative arrangements of standard fare and for the expressive vocals of Madelaine Taylor on traditional Scots such as "Birnie Bouzle" and "The Shearing." If you want to hear how this music sounded before voices were overdubbed and when musicians essentially played live in the studio until their money ran out, this recording is for you (vocal and instrumental).

Skyedance, **Alasdair Fraser and Paul Machlis (Culburnie):** The fiddle has been an important musical force in Scotland for more than three hundred years, as illustrated by the many manuscripts and tune collections going back to the early eighteenth century. Alasdair Fraser is a contemporary force for Scottish fiddle on both sides of the Atlantic. He has been especially dedicated to reuniting the music with the old social dances, particularly the old form of step dancing once enjoyed throughout the Highlands and Islands of Scotland and still popular in Cape Breton, Nova Scotia. The Cape Breton fiddle, preserving the old Highland style so removed from classically influenced bowing techniques, has also inspired his music. These passions initially truly came together in *Skyedance,* Alasdair Fraser's memorable first duo album with pianist Paul Machlis. Fraser's fiddle takes on some ancient dances and melodies from Gaelic vocal music with great feeling and fire. Together with the title tune, "The J.B. Reel" and "Harris Dance" have become classics of contemporary Scottish fiddling and help explain why Fraser's rhythmic playing style is much admired and imitated across Scotland and the United States (instrumental).

Stony Steps, **Matt Molloy (Green Linnet):** The Chieftains longtime flute player Matt Molloy offers collections of reels, jigs, and slow airs demonstrating why he is one of Ireland's most respected traditional musicians. Joined by Arty Mc-Glynn on guitar and Dónal Lunny on bouzouki, bodhrán, and keyboards, the album's pivotal piece is the air "The Parting of Friends" followed by a slip jig and the reel "Paddy Ryan's Dream." That poet Seamus Heaney penned the liner notes is an unexpected bonus (instrumental).

The Storm, **Moving Hearts (Son):** This is an album to be found in the record collection of many a musician, in addition to long-term Celtic music fans. Rock and jazz inspired, Moving Hearts was still very much an Irish music band and the first to bring tenor and soprano saxophone into an uilleann pipes and whistle-led lineup. Unfortunately, like other groundbreaking Irish lineups, this band didn't last long. The various members, including piper Davy Spillane and the ubiquitous Dónal Lunny on bouzouki, bodhrán, and synthesisers, soon traveled onward to new musical pastures. Meanwhile, recordings like this one, featuring the sublime set "The Titanic," continue to inspire and influence the many bands following in their wake (instrumental).

Tríona, **Tríona Ní Dhomhnaill (Green Linnet):** Originally released 1975, this recording is a solo introduction to one of the most arresting voices and influential keyboard players in Celtic music. Produced just before she helped shape the sound of The Bothy Band, the pure, youthful voice and gutsy harpsichord playing on this album also reveal the origins of Ní Dhomhnaill's elemental influence on the bands Touchstone, Relativity, and Nightnoise. From singing in Irish on "Na Gamhna Gaela" to big ballads such as "Here's to All True Lovers," this is a captivating album and a chance to hear the emergence of a widely recognized talent and important influence for today's Irish musicians (vocal).

Venus in Tweeds, **Shooglenifty (Greentrax):** Only the atmosphere at the band's live performances surpasses the wild sound of a Shooglenifty album. This debut launched the contemporary ceilidh vibe on an unsuspecting audience and won an international following for Shooglenifty. The title track is a great example of the band's irrepressible sound on what are mostly original tunes, and the arrangement of the more traditional set "The Tammienorrie" would leave even the fittest of dancers in a state of exhaustion (instrumental).

The Well Below the Valley, **Planxty (Shanachie):** Formed in 1973, Planxty pioneered new approaches to arrangement and instrumental combinations, giving Irish music a youthful appeal for the first time in the modern era. This album features voices that have shaped the sound of modern Irish traditional song. They belong to Christy Moore and Andy Irvine on such songs as the ditty "Cúnla" and the eerie "Well Below the Valley," paired with mesmerizing instrumentals, led by piper Liam O'Flynn on such tunes as the slip jig set "The Kid on the Mountain" and "An Phis Fhliuch" (instrumental and vocal).

Who Am I, **Dougie MacLean (Dunkeld):** Dougie MacLean's music crops up on movie soundtracks, television programs, and on the albums of country music luminaries. Meanwhile, he has been busy producing his own albums for many years, having created the Scottish label Dunkeld Records in the early 1980s. As such, this well-loved singer/songwriter has managed to forge an international profile without delivering his talents into the hands of a major record label. His music has clearly not suffered. Far from that, it thrives in the setting of his native Perthshire. In 2001, he took the bold step of inviting his twenty-one-year-old son, Jamie, to produce his next album. As he no doubt guessed it may, this gave his music a new energy, and the songs benefited from the treatments suggested by the younger MacLean. Highlights include "Not Lie Down," "Charlotte," and Jamie MacLean's own musical statement "Nothing to Do with It" (vocal).

The Words That Remain, **Solas (Shanachie):** Hitting full stride on this album, Solas carries on in the tradition of trend-setting Irish bands such as Planxty and Moving Hearts, but with a twist; Solas is a United States–based lineup. Seamus Egan grew up in Philadelphia and County Mayo, Ireland, and formed his original group around guitarist John Doyle and singer Karan Casey, who had relocated to the United States, and Irish American fiddler Win Horan. For this album, multi-instrumentalist Egan created a progressive, high-energy vibe around new tunes and songs from American and Irish sources. Guest vocals from Iris de Ment on "Song of Choice" and banjo artist Bela Fleck on "The Stride Set" help to create a significant statement and secure the place of Solas at the heart of today's contemporary Irish sound (vocal and instrumental).

EIGHT

The Language of Celtic Music

Celtic music comprises dozens of different instrumental and vocal forms. With several languages
to describe them, the atmosphere quickly becomes dense with
new words and concepts. Here are some that will reprise our
earlier topics and a few more that may come in handy as you
go on to investigate this music further.

Amhrán: "Song" in Irish, these were particularly commonly
sung after the breakdown of the bardic tradition.

An dro: A traditional dance tune from Brittany.

Bagad: Breton name for a pipe band.

Bard: An older term for musician or poet, often itinerant or
retained by nobility, who composes songs and music in honor
of patrons. Clan chiefs' bards had particularly high status and

195 ▪

were expected to memorize hundreds of stories, poems, or melodies.

Bellows-blown pipes: Any set of bagpipes in which the sound is created by air pumped from a set of bellows strapped to the elbow.

Binou: High-pitched Breton bagpipes, mouth-blown and with one drone.

Bodhrán: A simple handheld drum, held upright and played with one small stick or beater.

Bombarde: An oboelike traditional Breton instrument, and often heard being played in partnership with the binou.

Border pipes: *See* Lowland bagpipes.

Bothy ballad: Humorous, earthy songs written by male agricultural workers to describe farm life in the northeast of Scotland. Workers (unmarried men) gathered at "feeing" or hiring markets and then traveled to a farm for the season where they were housed in small huts and cottages called bothies.

Bouzouki: An eight-stringed Greek instrument, introduced into Irish music in the 1970s and now popular throughout Celtic instrumental music.

Button box: Irish button accordion.

Canntaireachd: A series of vocal sounds used by a piping instructor to convey music orally to a pupil. The legendary piping family of the Isle of Skye, the MacCrimmons, reputedly invented this ancient system.

Caoineadh: An Irish lament from the song tradition.

Cauld wind pipes: Another name for Scottish bellows-blown bagpipes.

Ceilidh: Gaelic word meaning "a visiting," originally used to describe an informal gathering in someone's home where music and storytelling might take place. Now the word is more commonly used to describe a community dance and style of traditional group dancing.

Ceol beag: Literally translated as "small music," Scottish pipe tunes of dance music and songs.

Ceol mor: Literally translated as "big music," the classical form of Scottish bagpipe music known as piobaireachd or pibroch.

Chanter: The fingered section of a set of bagpipes into which the reed is positioned. Beginners learn first on the chanter before being introduced to a full set of pipes.

Clarsach: A small Scottish harp.

Comhaltas Ceoltoiri Eireann: A movement founded in 1951 to generate enthusiasm and goodwill for Irish traditional music. More than six hundred branches now exist worldwide.

Concertina: A handheld instrument with buttons and bellows and an internal set of reeds that produce the notes when air passes across them. Similar to, but much smaller than, an accordion.

Couples de Sonneurs: Pairs of traditional singers or pipers from Brittany, often heard performing at a Breton fest noz.

Craic: A word used in Ireland and Scotland loosely meaning "good fun" and particularly associated with the music scene.

Crunluath: The third section of variations played in a piobaireachd before returning to the original tune, or "urlar."

Crwth: A traditional Welsh harp.

Dans Plin: A traditional dance from Brittany.

Diddling: A way of singing a tune, sometimes for children, using nonsense vocables to reproduce the melody and rhythm.

Drone: One of the wooden tubes or "stocks" tied into the bag of the pipes. In addition to the blowpipe and chanter, the Scottish Highland bagpipes have two tenor and one bass drone. These are propped across the left shoulder. (Also refers to the continuous background sound of the pipes, fiddle, or other instrument, particularly used as an atmospheric device in Scottish music.)

Eisteddfod: A cultural festival and competition in Wales.

Feis: Gaelic for "entertainment," a feis is a festival of tuition in traditional arts, with a particular emphasis on young people. The Feisean nan Gaidheal movement began on the Isle of Barra in 1981 and has now spread throughout the Highlands and Islands of Scotland.

Fest noz: A gathering with traditional dance and music held throughout Brittany in the summertime.

Fisel: A traditional dance from Brittany.

Fleadh Cheoil: A traditional music festival in Ireland.

Gaidhealtachd (or Gaeltacht): The geographical region in which the languages of Scots Gaelic or Irish are spoken.

Gaita: High-pitched bellows-blown bagpipes from Galicia.

Gavotte: A traditional dance tune from Brittany.

Grace notes: Decorative notes above or below the melody, heard especially in traditional singing, piping, fiddling, and flute and whistle playing.

Ground: The theme established at the beginning of a piobaireachd. *See also* Urlar.

Hardanger fiddle: The traditional Norwegian fiddle, with droning strings, also popular in Shetland fiddle music.

Highland: A version of the Scottish strathspey developed in Donegal, Ireland.

Highland bagpipes: The most recognizable of the bagpipes and the variety seen played in pipe bands the world over. Highland pipes comprise a bag made of animal hide, a blowpipe, two tenor and one bass drones, and the fingered pipe or chanter.

Hornpipe: A traditional dance tune of English origin, played in 2/4 or 4/4 time.

Jig: A traditional dance tune, most commonly played in 6/8 time, older than all other Irish dance tunes.

Kan Ha Diskan: The traditional Breton singing style of chant and counterchant, where singers trade the melody of the song back and forth with a characteristic overlap at the end of each phrase.

Lilting: A way of singing a tune using nonsense vocables to reproduce the melody and rhythm.

Lowland bagpipes: Similar in sound to the Highland bagpipes, but with less volume, these sets of bagpipes, also known as Borders pipes, are small, three droned, and bellows-blown.

Mod: Founded in 1892, this annual Scottish competition-based festival celebrates Gaelic language and culture through music, dance, drama, art, and literature.

Mouth music: The method of creating instrumental music by singing rhymes or even nonsense syllables to the melodies and rhythms of strathspeys, jigs, reels, etc. *See also* Puirt-a-beul.

Northumbrian bagpipes: Small, bellows-blown bagpipes associated with Northumberland in the northeast of England.

Orain mhor: Literally translated, it means "great songs," composed by bards to praise their patrons.

Piobaireachd (also pibroch): "Pipe music," the classical music of the Highland pipes composed as a theme with variations.

Pipe band: Massed bands of pipers and drummers, first established by Scottish regiments and then by civilian groups in the nineteenth century. The conventional setup uses one bass drum, two tenor drums, four to six side drums, and at least six pipers.

Planxty: An Irish tune written in praise of someone, often a patron. Planxties are associated with the compositions of Irish harper Turlough O'Carolan.

Polka: A traditional dance tune in 2/4 time, most commonly used in the set dancing of County Kerry and County Cork in Ireland.

Puirt-a-beul: Gaelic mouth music, using words and vocables to create dance music in the rhythms of strathspeys, jigs, reels, etc. The effect imitates the sound of the bagpipes. *See also* Mouth music.

Reel: A traditional dance tune in 4/4 time, originating in Scotland and most popular in set and step dancing.

Rond: A traditional dance tune from Brittany.

Scots snap: A distinctive feature of Scottish music in which a short, heavily accented note, followed by a longer one, creates a rhythmic skip in the music. In the case of Scottish fiddling, this is created by a sudden up-stroke of the bow and is most pronounced in a strathspey.

Sean nós: Literally translated, it means "old style," the ancient unaccompanied style of singing in Irish.

Session (also seisuin): An informal musical gathering, most often held in a pub or a private home.

Set: A traditional group dance, also a grouping of dance tunes played on any instrument.

Siubhal: Following the theme, this is the first round of variations of a piobaireachd.

Slide: A traditional Irish dance tune in 6/8 time, particularly associated with Counties Kerry and Clare.

Slip jig: A traditional dance tune in 9/8 time.

Small pipes: Another type of Scottish bagpipe, quieter still than the Lowland or Border pipes. Small pipes are similar in sound to the Northumbrian pipes but are played with the distinctive Scottish fingering heard in Highland piping.

Step dancing: A traditional dance form, performed solo or in a group, in which the feet tap out the dance rhythms of hornpipes, jigs, and reels.

Strathspey: A slow dance tune thought to have originated in the Spey Valley, this is a dance rhythm unique to Scottish music. Most often heard played on fiddle, it is recognizable for its built-in rhythmic skip.

Taorluath: The middle section of a piobaireachd.

TMSA: The acronym for the Traditional Music and Song Association of Scotland. This largely volunteer-run organization, formed in 1966 to foster the traditional arts, promotes festivals, concerts, ceilidhs, and the collection of traditional music for publication.

Travelers: The indigenous itinerant families of Scotland and Ireland, known at one time as "tinkers" (now pejorative), who travel the country performing seasonal farm labor and, at one time, repair work for the settled community. As they camped across the land, they would pick up songs and stories and in time became a great source of traditional balladry and storytelling.

Triple harp: The traditional harp of Wales, unique for its three rows of strings.

Trowie tunes: Tunes from Shetland believed to have been composed by fairies.

Uilleann pipes: The most complicated of all the bagpipes, these Irish bellows-blown pipes have a two-octave range. There are three different drones (bass, baritone, and tenor) and also thirteen regulators (closed pipes), allowing the piper to create harmonies and chords over the melody. *Uilleann* is Irish for "elbow."

Urlar: The theme, or ground, of a piobaireachd.

Waulking songs: Women's work songs, sung in Gaelic in the Hebrides of Scotland, to accompany the rhythmic work of "waulking" or shrinking the woven tweed cloth.

Resources for Curious Listeners

Like the music itself, the abundance and variety of related resources are increasingly easy to find. And just like the music, wading through the sheer choice of material now available can be a bit overwhelming. This collection of books, magazines, websites, retail outlets, and radio shows should help you explore it all further with ease.

Books

To learn more about Celtic music, its roots and branches, pick up some books. This library shelf includes a bit of everything on the subject.

The Ballad Book, **MacEdward Leach, editor:** This meticulously researched collection of 370 English, Scottish, and American ballads was edited by a leading American folklorist of the early twentieth century. The ballads are studied as a literary form in an extensive introduction examining the nature of the ballad. Notes on origins also accompany each song.

Celtic Music, **Kenny Mathieson, editor:** The well-known music writer and reviewer introduces a considered and carefully structured collection of writing on Celtic music. Music journalist Sue Wilson offers a typically well-written view of the road ahead, and Mathieson himself clears up misconceptions and myths about the genre.

Celtic Music: A Complete Guide, **June Skinner Sawyers:** Thoroughly researched, this is a comprehensive guide to the music, its history, and its influences. The author works her way through tunes, songs, dance styles, instruments, and musical developments, offering artist profiles, discographies, fascinating asides, and suggested resources. Sawyers doesn't shrink from expressing her opinion, making this a stimulating, enjoyable, and useful read.

Celtic Tides: Traditional Music in a New Age, **Martin Melhuish:** Cornish author Melhuish tells the story of the recent Celtic music boom through profiles and interviews with artists from Old World and new. The book was published as a companion to a CD compilation and video from Putumayo World Music and a documentary film produced by Hallway Entertainment. An extensive discography, festival listings, and even Irish music pub recommendations are all included.

The Celts, **Frank Delaney:** Anyone with an interest in the ancient history of the Celts will be well pleased with this account by best-selling author Delaney, published to complement a BBC series of six television documentaries. The author traces the Celts from their origins, through the flowering of their ancient culture, its eventual decline, and remarkable legacy. Lively, entertaining writing and the inclusion of four Celtic legends from Ireland's cycles of mythologies offset the academic and archaeological research.

The Chieftains: The Authorized Biography, **John Glatt:** The book is a must, of course, for any fan of the legendary Irish group. But it is also a great read for anyone with an interest in the recent history of Irish music. Here is a chance to learn how The Chieftains pioneered the idea of the traditional instrumental band and saw the potential for an international audience for Celtic music. The book is alive with anecdotes and humor, helping explain some of the tremendous appeal of Irish music in performance.

The Complete Irish Street Ballads, **Colm O Lochlainn:** Here is a substantial one-volume edition of Colm O Lochlainn's *Irish Street Ballads,* first published in 1939, and his *More Irish Street Ballads,* published in 1965 when the collector was 73 years of age. More than two hundred songs are printed and annotated here, with musical notation. O Lochlainn's short introduction gives a wonderful account of the role of the ballad in eighteenth- and nineteenth-century Ireland and is an insight into the discipline exerted by the collector who documents his source for each entry. The influence of radio and television grew between the publication of his first and second volume. O Lochlainn's commentary on this in his second introduction is optimistic and prescient, as he predicts that "mechanical entertainment" will only increase awareness of Ireland's heritage of song.

The Essential Guide to Irish Flute and Tin Whistle, **Grey Larsen:** Grey Larsen is a flute, whistle, and concertina player and recording artist, in great demand as a performer and teacher. A native of the American Midwest, he has studied with Irish American masters and legendary players in Ireland. His excellent "how-to" book is intended for Irish flute and tin whistle players at every level, from beginner to advanced, and it offers even more than that to anyone interested in uncovering the heart and soul of the music. Larsen looks into the history of the instruments and playing styles and offers an in-depth analysis of Irish music theory, addressing how to adapt Irish-style playing to the modern Boehm system flute. His is the first book to investigate the use of ornamentation in Irish music and to identify, explain, and notate these sophisticated techniques. Larsen has transcribed 27 tunes for his book, as played by 22 masters of Irish flute and tin whistle, and the 2 companion CDs included contain his musical examples and exercises. There is also computer software on the CDs.

Fair Melodies—Turlough O'Carolan: An Irish Harper, **Art Edelstein:** This book is an impressive package: the first biography of Carolan written in more than fifty years, the first discography of Carolan's compositions, and a fine CD containing twenty-one Carolan tunes recorded by guitarist Edelstein and friends. The book itself offers a fascinating insight into Carolan's time, a pivotal period in Irish history. It also documents the history of the Irish harp and includes interviews with some of its finest players, including the late Derek Bell.

Fiddles and Folk, **G. W. Lockhart:** This is an affectionate review of the work of some of the performers, collectors, and folk forces that have propelled Scotland's music around the world. The author avoids a formal approach to take a look at how individuals have risen to the forefront of the music, examining their lives, thoughts, and even their philosophies. His wide knowledge of the history and recent past of the music is warmed by his obvious pride in his country's culture and his musician's enthusiasm.

Notes from the Heart: A Celebration of Traditional Irish Music, **P. J. Curtis:** Musican, producer, radio broadcaster, playwright, and author P. J. Curtis is acknowledged as one of Ireland's leading champions of Irish and world music. He has produced more than forty albums for leading Irish artists, including Altan, Mary Black, Dolores Keane, Maura O'Connell, and Davy Spillane. All this puts him in a perfect position to chart the history of Irish music through the twentieth century, from the earliest recordings to its present day popularity. This book also explores the changing social context for the music and its cultural significance.

A Pocket History of Irish Traditional Music, **Gearóid Ó hAllmhuráin:** The author is an Irish historian, anthropologist, authority on Irish music, and also an all-Ireland concertina champion. His concise but expansive guide covers the history of the genre from early and Mediaeval times to the new millennium, including fascinating insights into such topics as the Norman influence on Irish music and dance in the twelfth century and a clear explanation of the recent restoration of musical traditions in Ireland. Tucked away at the back, but invaluable to any would-be Irish musician, O' hAllmhuráin includes a note on the etiquette of playing in an informal music session. Such gatherings may seem completely unstructured, but the social code is easily broken by the newcomer, and helpful advice is offered here.

The Scots Fiddle, **J. Murray Neil:** In this three-volume set, Neil has compiled an extensive selection of Scots fiddle music, along with a large number of historical biographies, anecdotes, tales, and traditions associated with the many melodies. This resource will prove invaluable for fiddle players who want to learn Scots tunes, including some previously unpublished compositions. It is also a fascinating browse for anyone with an interest in Scottish music and composers.

Scottish Traditional Music, **Nicola Wood:** This deceptively compact book provides a complete overview of Scottish musical traditions, from Bothy Ballads to Burns, and an in-depth description of the nation's traditional instruments of clarsach (harp), pipes, and fiddle. It is the perfect portable introduction.

The Scots Musical Museum 1787–1803, **Robert Burns and James Johnson, with an introduction by Donald A. Low:** Poems and original songs apart, Robert Burns was the foremost collector and arranger of traditional Scottish songs. *The Scots Musical Museum* was the product of this labor of love. These two volumes contain more than two hundred original and revised traditional songs, with the lyrics, melody, and simple bass line all included. Internationally renowned Burns scholar Donald A. Low provides a detailed introduction to a recent edition of this definitive collection. Anyone interested in one of Europe's most significant song collections, as preserved and extended by Burns, will want to have these two volumes on the shelf.

Tree of Strings/Crann Nan Teud, **Alison Kinnaird and Keith Sanger:** The first published history of the harp in Scotland traces its development from its earliest appearance in the eighth century to the present day. The story begins in the mists of bardic legend and follows the instrument to its revival in the nineteenth and twentieth centuries. The authors draw upon documents and private papers never before seen publicly and present a book of great historical detail for enthusiasts of the harp and traditional and early music in general.

Magazines/Journals/Newsletters

Let your special interest guide you through these publications. Learn about the emerging trends in the music, Celtic languages, new and established artists, cultures in which Celtic music is nurtured, and places to hear all this music as it should be heard: live.

Am Braighe
175 MacIntyre Road, Queensville, Nova Scotia, Canada B9A 1S6
www.ambraighe.ca
Scots Gaelic culture in Cape Breton has its own journal, covering history, music, genealogies, news, and events.

Bro Nevez
169 Greenwood Ave, B-4, Jenkintown, PA 19046
Not surprisingly, many Breton publications are written in either Breton or French. If neither is on your linguistic palette, you may appreciate this Breton newsletter written in the United States and covering a variety of topics of interest, including the language, culture, and music of Brittany.

Cleckan Press
The Thistle & Shamrock, PO Box 518, Matthews, NC 28106
thistle@npr.org; thistle.npr.org

This is the bimonthly newsletter of Cleckan, the Listeners' Association of NPR's weekly radio program *The Thistle & Shamrock*, produced and hosted by the author of this book. Guest articles by prominent Celtic musicians are a feature, along with CD competitions, program previews, and playlists.

Dirty Linen

PO Box 66600, Baltimore, MD 21239-6600
www.dirtylinen.com
This leading United States–based glossy publication covers Celtic music as part of a wider look at folk, traditional, and world music. Dirty Linen's website also features an extensive list of record label addresses.

fROOTS (formerly Folk Roots)

Southern Rag Ltd., PO Box 337, London, England N4 1TW
www.frootsmag.com
England's most influential folk magazine offers a glossy, monthly in-depth look at all roots-based music. Celtic music is set within the context of the broad British Isles and World Music scene. The magazine's website offers a monthly Internet radio program structured around the current issue's featured and reviewed music.

Golwg

PO Box 4, 13 Stryd Y Bont, Llanbedr Pont Steffan, Cardiganshire SA48 7LX, Cymru
The Welsh-language magazine is published weekly after a recent re-launch featuring a new design and larger format. It is available over the counter in Wales at some newsagents and Welsh-language shops.

Irish America Magazine
875 Sixth Avenue, Suite 2100, New York, NY 10003
www.irishamerica.com
Articles of news, views, and culture, from the Irish American viewpoint, are presented in this bimonthly magazine. The editorial board has an obvious interest in music, honoring many musical heroes in its annual Top 100 edition.

Irish Music Magazine
11 Clare Street, Dublin 2, Ireland
www.mag.irish-music.net
This monthly magazine is distributed worldwide and provides international listings of Irish music festivals, along with news, reviews, and features about the traditional and folk music of Ireland.

The Living Tradition
PO Box 1026, Kilmarnock, Ayrshire KA2 0LG, Scotland
www.folkmusic.net
Internationally distributed, this glossy bimonthly publication features news, reviews, and information from the world of traditional music, with a special emphasis on the Scottish scene.

The Scottish Banner—A' Bhratach Albannach
249 Main Street, Dunedin, FL 34698
(Canadian office: PO Box 724, Niagara Falls, ON L2E 6V5)
scottishbanner@aol.com, www.scottishbanner.com
Aimed at exiled and home-based Scots for nearly three decades, the newspaper claims to be the largest outside Scotland with a Scottish focus.

Scottish Folk Directory

Blackfriars Music, 49 Blackfriars Street, Edinburgh EH1 1NB, Scotland

www.scottishfolkdirectory.com

Of interest to enthusiasts and musicians alike, this annual directory lists and details everything imaginable about the Scottish folk music scene.

Scottish Life Magazine

87 Highland Avenue, Hull, MA 02045

www.scottishlife.org

This coffee-table quarterly is a collection of articles overviewing Scottish life and culture in general. Scottish music in its broad sense is regularly included.

Sounding Strings

PO Box 12508, Banchory, AB31 6WB, Scotland

Enthusiasts of the small harp have their own quarterly newsletter.

Taplas

182 Broadway, Roath, Cardiff CF24 1QJ, Wales

mail@taplas.freeserve.co.uk, www.taplas.co.uk

Taplas is a bimonthly magazine designed to keep its readers connected to the folk and traditional music scene as it unfolds in Wales. Each April/May issue is supplemented with a Festival Guide, and a complimentary CD is included every June/July.

Treoír

165 Fernly Park Drive, Alpharetta, GA 30022

www.comhaltas.com

The quarterly journal of Comhaltas Ceoltóirí Éireann is

available free of charge to all Comhaltas members and provides information on music sessions, festivals, and contests. Comhaltas is a social movement and provides a great way to connect with other Irish musicians the world over.

Websites

The rise of the World Wide Web has been a boon for independent record labels, artists, and music festivals. Now everyone has an opportunity to get information and downloadable music disseminated on an equal footing. Artists who are not signed to any record label, and who have never toured North America, can develop a following for their music, even offering mp3s. Well-established artists use websites to keep fans updated on tour dates, new releases, and more. You can track down much of what you may be looking for by conducting searches. Still, here are a few general sites that will interest you in the meantime and provide you with more links than you'll be able to follow in a leisurely afternoon of browsing.

Beag air Bheag (www.bbc.co.uk/alba/foghlam/beag_ air_bheag): BBC Scotland's Gaelic web-based resource center contains useful language and Gaelic culture links.

Celtic Roots (www.bbc.co.uk/scotland/musicscotland/ celticroots/): BBC Scotland's traditional and Celtic Music site offers downloads, reviews, sessions, gig guides, and more.

Ceolas (www.ceolas.org): This is the home of Celtic music on the web since 1994 and a complete online Celtic information resource center, including links to many related organizations.

Coop Breizh (www.coop-breizh.com): An online resource center, this Breton music site is run by the Coop Breizh record label.

Comhaltas Ceoltóirí Éireann (www.comhaltas.com): The society to promote traditional Irish arts offers information on where to hear live traditional Irish music, a selection of archives, and a virtual session.

Folkmusic.net (www.folkmusic.net): Provided by *The Living Tradition* magazine, this site is dedicated mainly to the folk and traditional music of the British Isles and Ireland. Read article archives and learn about the Tradition Bearers project.

Footstompin' Music (www.footstompin.com): Run by the Footstompin' record label, this site offers the opportunity to read, discuss, and listen to the news, views, articles, and CDs of Celtic music from Scotland.

Guide to Music in Brittany (www.breizh.net/saozneg/index.asp): Managed by the Breton language society, this site offers a good variety of resources on Breton music.

The Thistle & Shamrock (thistle.npr.org): NPR's Celtic Music radio program offers a resource featuring upcoming program descriptions and recent playlists. There are also extensive transcripts of many artist interviews, article archives, links to musician and record label sites, and a discussion board. NPR's first free music download was offered on this site in 2003.

TMSA (www.tmsa.info): Site of the Traditional Music and Song Association of Scotland, a group dedicated to promoting, preserving, and presenting Scotland's musical heritage. Traditional music listings and complete guide to Scottish music festivals are good resources here.

Tullochgorm (www.tullochgorm.com): Dedicated to traditional Scots Gaelic music in North America, this resource offers extensive background information on the music and information on Canadian Celtic artists.

Stores/Mail-Order Outlets

Gone are the days when you needed to don a pith helmet and secure the services of a local guide to lead you to Celtic music you could actually purchase. The genre secured its own section in many national and provincial recorded music outlets by the early 1990s; however, there are still some places where in-house knowledge and range of available stock are unsurpassed.

Blackfriars Music
49 Blackfriars Street, Edinburgh, EH1 1NB, Scotland
scotfolk@compuserve.com
Here is a place to come if you want to deal in used bagpipes. They also stock new instruments, books, and CDs.

Briathra-Amhran-Ceol
www.briathra-amhran-ceol.scotnet.co.uk
The name translates as "Words-Song-Music," and there's a wide selection of Celtic material available for purchase as well as CDs and mp3s along with books. Enthusiasts of Welsh music in particular will be well pleased with its strong representation here. (This is the only website that directs its

revenues into supporting promotion and tuition of the Gaelic language in Scotland.)

Celtic Note
14–15 Nassau Street, Dublin 2, Ireland
www.celticnote.com
Celtic and classical music from Ireland and Scotland are the speciality here, along with books, musical instruments, and videos.

The Celtic Trader
645-G Pressley Road, Charlotte, NC 28217
www.celtictrader.com
This is a long-established store with a large stock of Celtic recordings and a wide knowledge of the music.

Claddagh Records
2 Cecilia Street, Temple Bar, Dublin 2, Ireland
www.claddaghrecords.com
This record store of note stocks a wide range of traditional recordings, along with songbooks and Irish music reference materials.

Coda Music
12 Bank Street, The Mound, Edinburgh EH1 2LN, Scotland
www.codamusic.co.uk
Coda offers a very wide selection of acoustic and roots-based recordings, especially Scottish music.

Elderly Instruments
1100 N.Washington, Lansing MI 48901
www.elderly.com

This is a highly regarded mail-order service for acoustic musical instruments and much more.

Tayberry Music
760 Ragin Lane, Rock Hill, SC 29730
www.tayberry.com
Since 1987, Tayberry has been providing mail-order service in Celtic music recordings, books, and pennywhistles.

Radio On-Air and Online

Public radio in your area may offer a good service of local and syndicated programs featuring Celtic music. If not, thanks to cyberspace, other public service broadcasters have developed new ways of reaching you, wherever you may be. Tune into the finest in Celtic radio from the United Kingdom, Ireland, the United States, and Canada via your computer. Just check these broadcasters' home pages for live streaming times and program archives.

BBC Radio 2
www.bbc.co.uk/radio2
The most listened-to radio station in the United Kingdom combines popular music and culture and has a strong commitment to acoustic music. Follow the link to Mike Harding, whose show can be located under the Folk and Country program selector and features the best folk and acoustic music, with an interest in music from Celtic roots. The program streams live each week on the Radio 2 website and is archived in the week following each broadcast.

BBC Radio Scotland
www.bbc.co.uk/radioscotland

Scotland's national station presents a variety of one-off programs and documentaries touching on many aspects of Scottish music and culture. Two ongoing weekly broadcasts are well worth tuning in: *Celtic Connections* and *Travelling Folk*. *Celtic Connections* is a blend of classic Celtic music and newly released material placing Celtic sounds in the context of musical traditions from around the globe. Gaelic singer and harper Mary Ann Kennedy is the presenter of this broad-minded program. The noted folk singer and guitarist Archie Fisher presents the long-established *Travelling Folk*. Each week Fisher samples from among the best in traditional and folk music and includes folk news, an events calendar, and a monthly review panel. Regular studio sessions feature top bands and rising names. Both programs stream live on the BBC Scotland website and are archived in the week following each broadcast.

BBC Radio Wales
www.bbc.co.uk/wales

This is the only broadcaster producing services in English and Welsh, exploring all aspects of Welsh news and culture. *Celtic Heartbeat*, Frank Hennessy's award-winning series, specializes in traditional and contemporary Celtic and acoustic music. Live sessions from studio guests are included.

CBC Canada
www.cbc.ca

Canada's national broadcaster presents *Musicraft*, a program tuning into the musical talent in Newfoundland and Labrador. The show broadcasts musical events from across the province, including the weekly *Folk Night at the Ship Pub* in downtown St. John's. Named after a parish in Waterford, Ireland, this Newfoundland town was heavily settled by Irish-speaking fishery workers in the eighteenth century. Today's young musicians can be heard tapping into the traditional tunes in circulation at the *Ship Pub* and beyond. Shows are streamed live on CBC Radios One and Two via Real Audio.

NPR's *The Thistle & Shamrock*®
www.thistle.npr.org

Hundreds of public radio stations across the United States air NPR's award-winning weekly program of traditional and contemporary music from Celtic roots. A full list of where and when to hear the show is available at the program's website, where there are also links to those stations, many of whom stream the program live on the web. Hosted by the author of this book for more than twenty years, each hour is produced in Scotland for distribution by NPR, but *Thistle* can also be heard internationally on NPR Worldwide via WorldSpace satellite radio, Cable USEN 440, and the American Forces Network, among others.

RTE Ireland
www.rte.ie/radio

Ceol Net is RTE's traditional music service on the Internet. The Irish national broadcaster has a remarkable archive of traditional Irish music and song, stretching back across decades of field recordings. Ceol Net offers a live continuous webcast based around hundreds of hours of Irish music.

WFUV 90.7 FM
www.wfuv.org

This Bronx-based radio station is renowned for a music mix in which the Celtic sound plays an important part. The commitment to its Irish audience dates back to the early 1970s, when the show *Ceol na nGael* debuted, hosted today by

Deirdre McGuinness and Frank McCaughey, and offering popular music, culture, and news from Ireland. Kathleen Biggins has hosted *A Thousand Welcomes* live every Saturday morning since the late 1980s. She covers Celtic music in the broad sense, with a special focus upon the New York Irish music scene and its keynote contributors: Cherish the Ladies, Eileen Ivers, and John Whelan. *Mile Failte* is Dr. Seamus Blake's show serving serious students of the Irish language. All of WFUV's locally produced Celtic programs are archived on the station's website.

Index